# Down On The Tree Farm

*by*

## Florence Hardesty

*For John Osborn and Jean Witte — Who keep me sparkling —*

*Florence Hardesty*

*Silver Tree Books*

# Down On The Tree Farm

## Table of Contents

# Acknowledgments

Many people contributed to the publication of this book and it is dedicated to them. My friend and colleague, Dr. Joanne Hall, urged that the stories I told over lunch be written and preserved. My husband, Verl Holden, supported my efforts and had no objection when he became the main character of the book. My daughters, Susan Irvine and Shevawn Hardesty, never doubted that I could write. Their confidence gave me courage. I am grateful to all the wonderful people who appear on these pages, those who are named and those to whom I have given pseudonyms. Kristi and Paul Holden, Ruby, Doris, Larry, Isidra, Javier, Ernesto, Jolie, Mark and all the others who gave me material, I thank you. I am especially grateful to Thorn and Ursula Bacon, whose editorial and publishing expertise made the book possible.

Thank you all for being part of this effort and for making my life on the tree farm full and exciting.

*Florence Hardesty*

# 1

## Down On The Tree Farm

This is not the classic tale of a city girl marrying a farmer and learning to cope with rural life. To begin with, I'm not a girl. I was fifty when I met Verl.

I grew up in rural western Pennsylvania in a house on a farm that had been in my mother's family since the late 1700s. My father sold insurance and had no interest in farming so Mother rented out the farm. Mother, who "escaped" farming when she went away to college, taught school.

I went to school with dedicated young men who had milked the cows before the school bus arrived and sometimes forgot to change their shoes. The scents that permeated that Pennsylvania class room prevented me from noticing what nice fellows they were.

My best girl friend, Eleanor, lived on a farm adjoining ours. I spent long days at Eleanor's, helping to can, render lard and snap beans so that my friend would be free to play with me. The little animals constantly being born were appealing. But they grew up and became big animals that demanded care. My impression of farm life was that it was very hard work.

I went to the city to be educated, married and settled down—in a housing development. A little more than ten years later, I was divorced and living in Cleveland with two small daughters. School and jobs took me to upstate New York. Finally—about the time my children were raised—I moved to Oregon.

My career had come to a dead end at a small liberal arts college in upstate New York. My older daughter, Susan, had finished college and was married. The younger one, Shevawn, was a junior. My only responsibility was my mother who had suffered a stroke and was in a near-by nursing home. I discussed my job offers with her and she was ready to move anywhere I chose.

I interviewed for jobs around the country, checking out housing and nursing homes at the same time I investigated the schools. A position at the School of Nursing at the Oregon Health Sciences University held the most promising possibilities. Moving to the Northwest was an adventure and I was ready for one. Mother's nursing home gave her a bon voyage party. On the way to the airport she remarked that most of the residents departed from the home in a hearse rather than an airport limousine.

In 1976 I became an associate professor of Mental Health Nursing and a year later I was named chairman of the department. I bought a house and found that in Oregon weeds grew at an alarming rate. I cleaned up my yard in the fall, fully expecting to be finished with yard work until spring. I wandered out in February to find that my flower beds were inundated by dandelions with roots two feet long—nasties that had grown since November. I sold the house and bought a condominium. It was obvious that I was not a candidate for "farm woman" of the year.

Although I knew no one in Portland when I moved, I soon made friends at the school. A camaraderie exists among nurses that is similar to that among soldiers. We have so many common experiences that we relate easily to each other. But these new friends were all female, and I enjoyed and needed male companionship.

I had never had difficulty meeting men. But now I was fifty and burdened with the sense that what I did in my personal life reflected on my professional role. It didn't seem appropriate for me to be attending singles' bars. The men I met at singles' clubs and dances had little in common with me and seemed threatened by my education. And I had long before learned that it destroys a professional woman's credibility if she flirts with the men she meets at work.

A dating service was advertising its services. After some trepidation, I decided that it could be the solution and I signed up. The service introduced me to three men and I enjoyed each for an evening. But they didn't meet my major private criterion: a man had to be the sort of person I would spend time with if he were a woman. In other words, it wasn't enough that he be male or that he  pick up the dinner check. He had to be an interesting and compatible person as well.

The fourth phone number the service gave me was Verl Holden's. I called him on a Wednesday evening, since I wanted to plan my weekend and I hated waiting for the phone to ring. We had a pleasant conversation and he told me about himself.

He had a wholesale nursery fifty miles south of Portland in Silverton where he raised ornamental trees and ground covers. He had married his college sweetheart, Alice, several weeks after he finished a tour of duty in the Air Force and they had been partners in the nursery business. They had twenty good years together in spite of the fact that she had been chronically ill during the last years. She had died several years before at the age of 42, leaving Verl with a difficult fourteen-year-old daughter, Kristi, and a ten-year-old son, Paul. He told me he had been devastated by the loss of his lover, friend, mother of his children, and business partner.

He went on to tell me that he had married shortly after her death and that the second marriage had been a disastrous mistake. His second wife, Betty, had two children also and it seemed as though no one in this combined family really liked or respected one another. To everyone's relief, the marriage was over in less than a year. He had emerged wiser, but again he was lonely.

I was impressed by his honesty. Other men I had met waited for several dates before telling me about their second marriages. And not one had ever said that he had been unwise in his choice and accepted responsibility for the mistake.

He told me he felt uncomfortable in singles' bars

and didn't have time to be involved in activities that might lead to his meeting someone. His solution, like mine, was to turn the "looking" over to a dating service. We made a date for Saturday. I hung up the phone feeling as though I had just talked with an old friend.

I got ready for our date thinking that it would be a success if I had one pleasant evening. I was not looking for a husband and I had learned not to expect too much from blind dates, even ones arranged by a dating service.

The doorbell rang and I opened the door. My first thought was, "He is handsome," followed by, "He looks like Daddy."

Verl is good looking. He has curly gray hair, merry green eyes and the muscular body of a man who does hard physical work. Over dinner I found that he was intelligent and witty. I also discovered that he liked bright women and found them stimulating and sexy. Usually I kept my brain hidden on first dates. It was wonderful to be able to discuss the day's news and even disagree on politics. We danced together as though we had practiced for years. When I told him I had opera tickets for the next month and asked him if he'd like to go, he said yes enthusiastically, then told me he had played in his college symphony and string quartet. Verl is five years younger than I am, but that seemed unimportant.

He told me later that when he left me that night he stopped at a phone booth to look up my name and address. Meeting me and my obviously liking him seemed too good to be true. He needed some outside evidence to confirm the reality of the evening.

We both were delighted that we had found the

companionship we had been seeking. Neither of us was interest in marrying again. We dated on Saturday nights for a few weeks. Then the frequency of our dating grew steadily until we were seeing each other Friday, Saturday, Sunday and Wednesday. He was managing a demanding business, doing most of the field labor himself, and raising Paul, now thirteen, and Kristi, who was seventeen. My job was also demanding. I was managing a twelve-member department, teaching classes, doing research, writing grants and developing a graduate program. It was a relief to have a full and satisfying social life and to have found this wonderful supportive friend.

Mother died six months after I met Verl. When I called to tell him, he came to Portland immediately to be with me, and asked if he could go with me to take mother's body back to Pennsylvania for the funeral. How glad I was to have him with me when I made that trip! My daughters and the family liked Verl immediately. He had further evidence that I was real. Everyone we met knew me, and they all called me by my childhood nickname, Flossie.

A year after we met, he proposed and we set a wedding date six months ahead. The question of where we would live was a major one. He said, "I could sell the nursery and teach horticulture."

"What do you want to do with your life?"

He said, "I want to put a beautiful blue spruce in every yard in the United States."

"Okay, that settles it. We'll live at your place and I'll drive to Portland to work."

"I'll try to make that as easy as I can for you."

As the plans for the marriage were made, unexpected stresses appeared. Verl's parents did not think this career woman from "nowhere" was the proper wife for their son. They thought he needed a woman who would help him in the nursery and be there to pack the children's lunches. My younger daughter, Shevawn, who had met and liked Verl, informed me that it would be too upsetting to attend our wedding. Later I learned that she felt as though I was deserting her to live a "Little House on the Prairie" life with my new family. This was totally unexpected from my logical daughter who had behaved like an adult since she was twelve. Verl's daughter, Kristi, who had thought I was just a nice woman her dad was dating, was upset by the prospect of our marriage. She was a senior in high school and her plans for after graduation, which she hadn't discussed with anyone, were to stay at home and keep house for Verl and Paul. She envisioned that she would be displaced.

Since our relationship was being conducted while we lived fifty miles apart, the logistics were difficult. Verl needed to be at the nursery early in the morning. He also felt he had to cook bacon and make bacon sandwiches for Paul's lunch, a daily act of fatherly love. Kristi was at a rebellious stage of her development and her choice of friends was questionable. He needed to be at home at night to offer the control of his presence.

When I spent the night at Verl's, I was uncomfortable in the children's presence in the morning. Even worse was meeting his father, who was arriving for work, in the driveway as I was leaving. The clothes I wanted to wear or the books I needed always seemed to be fifty miles away.

I had begun to rely on Verl for the little things that husbands usually do. I was on the East Coast for a conference when United Airlines went on strike. All flights, mine included, were cancelled. I got one flight to San Francisco and another to Seattle, 250 miles away from Portland. It was an exhausting and nerve-racking trip. On the flight to Seattle, the stewardess noted my mental state and prescribed free champagne. I arrived in Seattle at four in the morning, bleary eyed and not thinking too clearly. I called Verl and said, "Can you come and get me?"

He didn't tell me he had a truck due in that morning to take a load of trees to New York. Instead he got in his car, drove to Seattle, found me asleep in an airport chair and drove me to my condominium in Portland. He got a ticket for speeding and had a flat tire after he let me out. The truck was late and he arrived at the nursery in time to load it. I am still amazed that I made such an unreasonable request.

Three months after we had decided to get married, in the middle of shipping season, Verl thought that it was all too much hassle and called off the wedding. He did it over the phone. I was too furious to be heartbroken. I drove to Silverton to pick up the things I had left there and to vent my fury, face to face. I arrived as Verl was stepping out of the shower. A towel is not a good outfit to fight in. My Irish ancestors would have been proud of the verbal assault that I made on Verl. I added final emphasis by stamping on his bare foot.

Then I cried and we talked. We decided that the logistics of our relationship, the intensity of the emotional involvement without the security of marriage, and the nervousness of our relatives were making things difficult. The solution, we decided, was to get married. So we did, the following week.

What follows is an account of my adventures of the last twelve years, down on the tree farm.

# 2

## The Landscaper's Yard

You've heard about the problems of the shoemaker's children. Well, let me introduce you to the landscaper's yard.

My second date with Verl was for dinner at his home. I drove from Portland, with a copy of the directions to the farm on the dash board, anxious to observe the environment of this interesting man. I pulled in the driveway by a big greenhouse and there was my handsome date, standing in waist-high grass beside a modern house. Since the house sat in the middle of a circular drive, it was difficult to tell the front from the back, but the weedy part was the section designed by the architect as the front of the house.

The backyard was well landscaped and the glass walls on the east side of the house faced it. The front section faced west and had been planned with no windows. Verl had lived there fifteen years and somehow had never found a landscape design that met his standards for the front of the house.

We married on a Saturday a little more than a year after that second date. Since we both had to be at work on Monday, our honeymoon was one day long. We stayed at my condominium in Portland and spent the day strolling through Portland's Japanese Garden.

The seed of an idea was forming in Verl's mind. But it took more to move him. I planned a party several weeks after the wedding to introduce my new husband to my friends.

Suddenly there was a flurry of activity in the front yard. A 30-foot tall unusual-looking pine tree was planted on a mound. At the base of its roots, a small stone waterfall appeared, and water bubbled into a rustic kidney-shaped pool. A wooden walk with rails of rope was built, from the driveway, across the pool, to the entryway. A very old *cedrus atlantica pendulae* spread its blue weeping branches over the pool casting a reflection like an old woman. A golden hinoki cypress stood like a tall sentinel at the beginning of the walk, its gold-edged leaves glittering in the wind. Red-leafed Japanese maples provided a colorful statement and all around, among the azaleas, was Verl's precious bamboo collection. Golden koi flashed in the depth of the pool.

My friends were impressed with the beautiful Japanese garden in our front yard.

The fire insurance man liked it too. He had warned Verl that the weeds were a fire hazard and that he must remove them. I prefer to think the transformation was wrought in honor of our marriage.

One evening shortly after the party, I stood admiring my old lady tree by the pool.

Verl said, "Yes, it is a beautiful plant. It is worth about five hundred dollars."

"You'd never sell it!"

"Every plant on this place is for sale, if the price is right."

"Not that tree, or my *hinoki cypress*. Promise me, you won't sell them."

"Okay. Not for a while anyway."

Our first Christmas tree was a live one, a concolor fir. We planted it in the front yard and I watched it grow and grow—and grow. One day Verl said, "I have to dig that fir in the front. It's too big and I have a sale for it."

I sadly agreed, and watched the first Christmas tree of our marriage lifted from the ground and its roots balled up in burlap. Verl moved it out by the road for the truck to pick up. The town that had bought it paid him a healthy amount for the large tree. But then the town fathers changed their mind and canceled the order. Since the tree was already dug, Verl kept the money.

The balled tree sat by the road. The first two years it looked sick, but it struggled to live. Then someone dumped sawdust around its roots and it began to grow again. Someday, someone will want a 30 foot tree and it will already be partially dug. I've tried to stop being sentimental about that tree.

Verl's bamboo (all 45 varieties) is extremely prolific. It invades every space in the garden. It crept into my English garden where I had planted the flowers of my childhood—roses, lilacs, peonies and iris.

I asked Verl, "What can I use to kill that damn bamboo that is strangling my roses? Is *Roundup* enough or will I need a stronger herbicide?"

"Oh, don't kill it. When it is time I'll dig it out and get thirty dollars a plant for it."

So if you come to visit, don't be surprised to see puny roses and healthy bamboo in my garden.

Verl planted a row of pine between our back yard and the loading yard. They had long graceful needles and sensuous columnar shapes. I loved to sit on the patio in the evening and watch the wind move their slim branches. Verl had warned me when he planted them that they would get too large to stay there and would have to be moved.

One sleepy summer morning I opened the patio door and headed out to get the morning paper. I stopped dead in my tracks. My beautiful hedge of trees was gone! They were laying on the ground, their roots encased in huge balls of hard round earth. Our small dark-haired employees were swarming over them, rolling the root balls this way and that as they wrapped them tightly in burlap. Even in the horror of my loss, I could not help but admire the skill and strength of our workers.

I rushed out to where Verl stood by a semi-truck. "My trees!"

"Yes, dear. I got $300 apiece for them. They were getting too big anyway. I'll plant you another hedge."

He hasn't yet, but the trees did pay for a trip to

# Holland.

# 3

## The Contract

How can one be sure that the marriage one is planning will be happy? I've worked as a marriage counselor and mental health expert for 25 years and I don't know the answer. It isn't enough to be passionate about each other, but without passion the relationship is flat and uninteresting. It isn't enough to have all the logical reasons for marrying and all the reasonable criteria met, but it would be foolish to embark on a life-long contract without logic and reason on one's side.

You should know each other well and like each other, but even people who have known each other for years discover strange differences after marriage. Marriage is always risky—but so is life—and luck plays a role in bringing the right elements for happiness together.

Verl's ethnic heritage is English, Irish and Scots-Irish, and so is mine. That helps with the ways that we approach problems, different but familiar. When I am angry, I usually let the object of my anger know and try to work it out. Verl doesn't say anything. He just waits and gets even—like my brother does. He has a long memory and doesn't easily forget a wrong—like my father. There are times when I wish he would behave differently, but his behavior is never incomprehensible.

When we decided to get married, we made an appointment with an attorney, Verl's attorney, to sign a prenuptial agreement. Was this the powerful man protecting his business from a potential gold digger? Sure. And it was also a woman who wanted to be sure her children received what she had accumulated. We were both pleased with our "what's yours is yours and what's mine is mine" agreement. Our wills reflected the same philosophy.

Then after seven years I bought my farm and Verl contributed to the purchase of a property that would go to my daughters. We made new wills. The house and farm where we live will be inherited by Verl's children but all our children will inherit the business. Since then we have bought another farm and a house for our employees which are in both our names.

We keep our bank accounts separate and are free to make all but major purchases, things like a farm or a house, without consulting each other. I trust that if Verl wants to buy a tractor or a truck he needs it. He chuckled a little when I spent almost $2,000 for lavender jade beads (especially when the jewelry store sent home a bottle of champagne for him), but it was my affair and my debt. (The beads lost a little of their luster after the first twelve payments.)

I suppose the essence of our financial arrangement is that we trust the other has good judgement. I pay the hospital insurance and he pays the car and house insurances. He pays for the food and I shop and cook. He pays the cleaning lady and I pick up after him and do the laundry. We borrow from each other and write checks to pay the other. Our families think we are very strange when they see us doing this. Verl pays for the weekly Friday night movie and dinner, and I buy season tickets to the symphony, opera and plays. He pays for some vacations and I pay for others.

It all has happened easily and without strain or effort. There are times when I state my case and he listens. I wanted to retire from my job as a nursing professor but would not until I had an agreement that we would keep the cleaning lady. I did not want to exchange a high-paying position for a menial one. I volunteered to add the cooking and grocery shopping to my list of duties. Before I retired, he cooked on the week days when I got home late.

Since both of us have done the cooking, we are remarkably free of critical comments about the other's creations. We are held in check by the knowledge that he who kicks, cooks. Dishes are a joint project.

The outside work, garbage and mud rooms are Verl's responsibility.

I insisted that I have one room of the house that would be mine alone. I wanted to have a study where I could retreat and work without interruption. Verl agreed and I was awarded the family room which contained Paul's pool table. There was a door between the family room and the breakfast room, but it was relatively private.

I saw clients for marital counseling and psychotherapy in my study. Having a small private practice enlivened my teaching and enabled me to keep my licenses active. In order to have more privacy, we closed off the door between the study and the breakfast room and made a door leading directly outside. We also soundproofed the wall between the two rooms. I practiced until a year ago. Now my study is where I write, free from any disturbance.

A marriage between two middle-aged people has fewer problems than the marriage of two young people who are establishing themselves in careers and raising children. I'm sure we would have had more difficulty if we had married earlier in our lives. Aside from that, I'm not sure what has made it so easy for us. We have been blessed with a spark between us. It enables us to find such pleasure in each other's company that none of the little irritations or inconveniences that the relationship brings are worth fretting about. So we discuss a problem when it arises, solve it and go back to concentrate on the joy we find in the other's presence.

Since I am unable to name the reason for our happiness, I conclude that it is beyond reason. Are we blessed? Is it luck? (My mother always said I had lots of luck.) Whatever the reason, I feel profound gratitude that I have had these years with Verl.

# 4

## Mr. Bang

Shortly after we were married I discovered a peculiar aspect of Verl's personality. We were on a trip east to visit my relatives and friends. I wanted to introduce my new husband to all the people who are important to me and he was eager to know them. Paul, was with us. It was not a classic honeymoon, but an important occasion nevertheless.

We were sitting the the living room at the home of Shevawn's boyfriend, George. George, his brother and several young men were there—a perfect audience. Someone asked Verl about the nursery and the conversation turned to the task of removing large trees. From there it evolved onto the joy of blasting.

Verl's green eyes sparkled and he leaned back to regale the group with his "blasting tales." He began with the story of how he had blown a stump at the nursery he managed when he got out of the Air Force.

The nursery was the one where he had been introduced to horticulture when he was a skinny seventh grader eager to earn money to pay for his violin lessons and new bicycle. The farm was spread along the bottom land near the Willamette River. It produced fruit trees, nursery ornamentals and filberts. Verl had many other jobs as he worked his way through high school and college, but this first nursery was always the most important one. It was the one that had set the direction of his life's work.

Verl graduated from college and went off to the Air Force and Japan. He returned to marry Alice and began work as a nurseryman. His first boss was eager to hire him. He and Alice moved into a tiny rent-free house on the nursery. Alice was an accountant at a local savings and loan. Their long-term goal was to own their own business and they began saving money to achieve that. In the meantime, Verl was happy to be back at the nursery where he began.

The man who owned the nursery died a short time after Verl began working there and his daughter inherited the business. She had no interest in the nursery other than as a source of income and was relieved when Verl agreed to stay on as manager.

He was in his early twenties, weighing only one hundred and forty pounds. His curly hair was almost black and the brows that arched over his green eyes were dark. When I see pictures of him at that age, I always look at his ears expecting them to be pointed. I bought a figurine of the young god Pan once because it reminded me of Verl. A woman who cleaned for us once told me that she hurried by the picture of young Lieutenant Holden that hung in the hallway because she was afraid the imp in the picture would goose her.

Verl worked very hard on the nursery but he and Alice found time to play as well. Both were excellent shots, and the ducks that lived in the shallows of the river and feasted on the filbert orchards were easy prey. He trained bird dogs and had a boat. They entertained their college friends and even disasters like the frequent floods became adventures.

It is strange that I can almost remember young Verl. I didn't know him then, of course. The stories that he tells have such vividness that I feel as though I were there. He was older, heavier and gray that day in George's living room telling his blasting story, but young Verl was present beneath the middle-aged facade.

He described a glorious June day. Oregon's damp, cool climate causes Oregonians to appreciate perfect summer days, days when the sky is cloudless, a gentle breeze stirs the trees and, off to the east, the Cascade range is purple against the sky. Verl and several workers were leveling land to build a new greenhouse. Right in the middle of the space was the stump of an old fir tree. It was six feet across and even though the tree had been cut several years before the roots were solid and deep in the ground. Verl considered his options. They could saw it up and drag the stump out with a tractor, one piece at a time, and then dig down to get at the roots. A bulldozer could push it out, but they would have to hire one and perhaps wait for it to come, Or he could set a charge under the stump and blow it out.

A road crew working on the road that ran past the nursery was using a bulldozer. The had parked their monster machine in an orchard several hundred yards away and were eating lunch.

Verl made the decision, he would blow out the stump. The owner was away so she wouldn't be disturbed by the noise.

He dug under the stump and prepared the explosive. He mixed fertilizer, pellets of ammonium nitrate, with diesel oil to produce an inexpensive explosive mixture. He poured just the right amount under the stump. This mixture requires a strong jolt to set it off. A stick of dynamite served that purpose. He hooked the dynamite to a blasting cap and strung three hundred feet of wire to the battery that would set off the cap, the dynamite and the fertilizer.

He warned the workers about what was goingt to happen. He ran out to talk to the bulldozer crew. They had experience with blasting and apparently thought Verl's admonition to move from their spot in the orchard was overly cautious.

Everything was ready. Verl pressed the button. Kaboom! The large stump disintegrated and went skyward in a cloud of dust. When blasting the rule is to look up so you can see what is about to fall on you. Verl followed the rule.

When the dust cleared, he saw the road crew crawling out from under the bulldozer with surprised expressions on their faces and wearing their lunches on their work clothes.

Verl looked toward the house and saw a huge hole in the screen door leading to the living room.

He inspected the living room and discovered that a leg and been blown off a buffet by a piece of bark that had entered through the screen. On the grand piano, a crystal hurricane lamp had shattered into a pile of shards.

He hastily repaired the buffet with glue and varnish and never told the owner that it had been damaged. New screen was immediately found for the door. But he left the glass where he found it.

"What happened here?" the owner asked when she returned home.

"Oh, we took out that stump over there," said Verl. "I guess the blast broke your lamp."

A true nurseryman's daughter, she understood that blasting is an imprecise art and that was the last on the subject. However, it did provide the first of a long series of blasting stories that Verl told with delight.

As his stories unfolded, the men laughed along with him. I sat horrified at Verl's glee, a glee that completely overshadowed the reality of danger.

When we were alone I made him swear that he would never do any blasting at the nursery when I was there. "I don't want to go out there and find you in pieces."

He promised to obey my admonition.

After we returned home, I began to overhear phone calls from the neighboring farmers. They went like this:

"Say, Verl, I have a big stump out by my loafing shed. It's too close to get a cat in there and too big to blast out. But I was wondering, could I put a little charge under it, just enough to break it up, so I could drag the pieces out with the tractor?"

Verl would answer with a delighted lilt in his voice, "Sure, you could do that. Do you want me to come over and help you?"

"If you have the time that would be great."

At social events whenever the subject of dynamite came up, and it does often in a farming community, Verl, eyes bright, held the crowd enthralled with his reminiscences of blasts. That is when I christened him "Mr. Bang."

He assured me that he was careful. I recognized that dynamite is a useful tool on a farm, and he did have an explosives license. It was hard for an ignorant urbanite to argue with a rural expert. But there would be no more blasting stories, I told myself.

We had been married seven years when I decided to sell my condominium in Portland. My brother and I had inherited the farm in Pennsylvania. It had been strip-mined and its only current value was sentimental. I had resisted selling, citing the possibilities for future development. But I finally acquiesced to my brother's pleas and sold it. For the first time since I was twenty I owned no property.

I found a neglected 30-acre farm two miles down the road from Verl's nursery and bought it. Although it was in my name, Verl contributed a substantial sum so I could pay cash for it. He began to make it into a beautiful farm with the enthusiastic joy with which he tackled projects.

The farm had a small house on it. We fixed it up and rented it to a nice young couple, Mary and Hank. We drilled an irrigation well. There was a 12-acre pasture that had never been used for crop land. Verl drained it and cut 25 large oak trees that had provided shade for the pasture. The plan was to plant a filbert orchard to provide me a with regular income. Since it takes ten years for filberts to be commercially profitable, Verl planted nursery stock between the rows. As the filberts matured the nursery material would be sold. This kind of planning made the farm profitable immediately. Shrewd, careful farmer, that man I married!

Of course there were those 25 oak stumps to be removed. There were too many to saw up and dig out—it would take the workers weeks to do that. If we hired a bulldozer it would compact the soil so the roots of the trees we would be planting would be less able to breathe. (Yes, roots must also breathe.) The best solution would be to blow the stumps out of the ground. How could I protest blasting when Verl had so generously made my farm valuable? So I consented, admonishing him to be careful.

Verl likes to blast on Sunday. There are no employees around and not many motorists passing by to be startled by the big bang or showered with dust. He spent one Sunday at my farm and twenty stumps were moved out of the earth and broken into manageable pieces. Another Sunday and he would be finished and our men could get the ground ready for planting.

That last Sunday Verl had almost finished blasting. It had gone without a hitch and only one stump remained. It was in the barnyard, 250 feet from the house. The tree had been cut before we bought the place, but the stump was firm with no sign of rot. When the sheep were down at that farm, the lambs loved that stump. One at a time they would climb on it and challenge their fellows to butt them off. It was almost a shame to take it out, but farmers are practical.

Verl stood and stretched as he looked back over his work. He thought about how hard it must have been for the early settlers to dig out the huge Douglas fir stumps. Life now was certainly easier for farmers.

He poured the oil soaked pellets of ammonium nitrate into the hole. The 80-pound sack was now empty. Then he put in the dynamite and blasting cap. He was finishing early and that was good because we had been invited out for dinner that evening.

He looked up and down the road. There were no cars. The fields adjoining the farm were deserted. All clear. Verl touched the battery—and then looked up.

Bang!

Clods of earth and dust filled the air and settled back to the ground. The job was finished. Suddenly he heard a shout and, peering through the dust, he saw our tenant, Hank, running toward him.

I was at home, listening to Mozart and sewing when the phone rang.

"Florence." Not the usual dear or honey.

"What's wrong?"

"Well, there's been a little accident," Verl said

"Anyone hurt?"

"No, but Mary is pretty upset. Come on down."

I jumped in my car and drove the two miles to my farm. What could have happened? I was fond of this newly married couple who were my tenants. Hank was employed by the state doing road maintenance and Mary worked for an insurance company. They were saving to buy their own home but in the meanwhile they took wonderful care of my house.

The neat farm house looked fine to me as I hurried through the well-kept yard. The door was open. When I stepped through it, I waded into four inches of water. Mary was sweeping this lake out of the kitchen door. She was wearing a pink flowered bathrobe and her feet were bare. Her soft blond hair was plastered to her cheeks by perspiration.

"What happened?"

"The bedroom. Look."

I splashed into the bedroom. There in the middle of what had been the waterbed was a 250 pound stump. One root skewered the waterbed to the floor and rested on the ground underneath the house. The bedroom ceiling was gone and the bright blue sky showed through the hole in the roof. The contents of the waterbed lapped gently against the baseboards and flowed into the closet.

Verl stood by the bed. My face demanded an explanation. "The stump was at least 250 feet from the house. The last one. I guess the roots were rotten. I must'a used too much ammonium nitrate."

Explanation given, he and Hank tackled the problem of getting the stump out of the house. Hank, a stocky man, whose blond curls give him an unexpectedly angelic look, wore a dazed expression. Finally the men hoisted the stump up and tossed it out of a window.

I went to help Mary. She wasn't emotionally upset, she was mad. My services a a psychiatric nurse weren't needed but she did accept my offer to help clean up the mess.

She had been reading the Sunday paper and dozing on the couch when the tree dropped in. She and Hank had skipped church that morning because she had been tired after a bad week at work. Hank had been watching the blasting through the bedroom window. He

had good reflexes. When he heard or saw the stump coming, he had moved so quickly he put his elbow through a plaster and lath wall.

I was too upset with the destruction to be mad and too grateful that there had been no injuries to complain. We moved the dry clothes from the bedroom closet into the guest room and rescued the contents of the lower dresser drawer before they became soaked. Shoes were lined up on the front steps to dry in the sun. The punctured water bed mattress was pitched out of the window after the stump. It was followed by the ruined sheets and bedspread. Verl had gone to the nursery to get the shop vac and one of the large rolls of plastic that he uses to cover greenhouses. He was on the roof tacking plastic over the entire structure. I was using the shop vac to suck up the water from the carpet. Most of it had been swept out the door or drained into the hot-air registers in the floor (to cause more problems later). Then Hank's parents arrived.

Oh boy, I thought, now we'll hear a lecture on safety.

Hank's mother is a Mennonite. She was dressed in a long-sleeved dark dress and wore a tiny lace cap over the prim bun at the back of her head. She began soaking up water from the carpets with bath towels.

"Blasting is sort of funny," she said.

Funny? I kept on sweeping.

"One time Dad and I hired a man to take out a stump for us. He came and got it all ready and—puff—there went the machine shed."

I loved that proper little woman.

The next day Verl hired a carpenter and the following day the roof and bedroom were as good as new.

The day after the blast, Mary went shopping with the cash Verl had given her and bought a new waterbed, sheets, comforter and carpet. (We are still using the ones they replaced as cleaning cloths and door mats.) Verl didn't turn a claim in to the insurance company.

Mary and Hank lived in the house for several more years. Rents in the area went up markedly but I never raised theirs.

It took a whole day for me to find any humor in this incident. But as soon as it began to surface, Verl, whose eyes turn cold gray when he is issuing a warning, said, "Don't you dare tell anyone!"

I tried, honest, to keep the story secret, but it got around the community without my help and I had to set the record straight.

Mr. Bang the mad dynamiter, has not been around for a while. I do miss his boyish joy in making a big blast—and his stories about it—but I'm glad he is gone.

# 5

## Do Drop In

When I married Verl, I moved into his house. This
was not without some sacrifice. I had been the one who
insisted that we make our home at Verl's house. I
agreed without reservation to drive to my job in
Portland. That only made sense. But it was hard to
move my precious things into his home and try to make
a nest in a strange house among another's belongings.

My dream house had always been a Cape Cod
colonial and my furniture would have fit perfectly

there. I had been collecting oriental rugs, paying for them month by month, and I owned many original paintings. I had inherited antiques from my mother and the rest of my furniture was reproductions. I loved deep roses, reds and blues.

Verl's house is modern. A friend of his had drawn the plans as an assignment for a master's degree in architecture. It was planned to fit the site and is the kind of house you would expect to see in California. I love the windows that cover the east wall of the living room, dining room and kitchen. They extend from the floor to the 12 foot ceiling, admit the morning sun and let us see the Cascade range. On clear days and at dawn you can see the snow-covered peak of Mt. Hood, sixty miles northeast. The same windows that permit this view make the living room chilly in winter. We seldom sit in there at night because it is so open.

Verl's furniture was conservative modern and he had an orange carpet and drapes of the same color chosen by his second wife. The living room is paneled in cedar, but the dining area and hall were papered with orange and white vertical stripes, stretching from the floor to the high ceiling.

How could I live there? I wondered that all the time we were courting. I hate orange—it makes my skin look green. As time went on and Verl became more important to me, I played a little game with myself at night while I waited for sleep. I would mentally place my furniture in his house, hang my pictures on his walls and struggle with the decorating problems engendered by two incompatible tastes.

I found the solution when I was looking for something in a closet at his house. Back in a corner I discovered some beautiful wood block prints that Verl had brought from Japan. They had never been hung. He gave me permission to have them framed, and I did, with narrow gold frames and soft blue mats. He liked the oriental motif and my belongings would blend very well with it. I had found a bridge to combine our tastes. Love had triumphed over decorating.

I got rid of the orange-stripped wallpaper immediately after moving into Verl's home. The drapes took a little longer.

One day the cleaning woman said, "Florence those drapes are dusty. We should take them down and shake them.

"I know they're dusty. The sun is rotting them too. I'm afraid if I take them down they will fall apart."

And this wise woman answered, "Yes."

I replaced them with soft blue, translucent blinds. A few years later I replaced the orange living-room carpet with a parquet floor and a beautiful deep-blue Chinese rug. The bedroom floor still has orange carpet, but it is covered with oriental rugs and I hardly know it is there.

Verl is very proud of our home and together we have added art, original bronze and wood sculptures. I would hate to move from here, even if we were to build a Cape Cod colonial.

The roof is a problem we have not yet conquered. The architect planned a butterfly roof. Think of squashed-down M. The roof is almost flat but it has two low peaks with a valley between. Beams run through the house at eight-foot intervals decorating the vaulted ceilings and extending through the walls or windows to support the wide eaves.

In Oregon, it rains from the second week of September until June. Plants thrive and roofs get wear. On our roof the valley between the peaks becomes a

stream when it rains and the water drains off into ingenious down-spouts at either end. Well...it is supposed to drain off.

The first six years I lived with Verl the roof leaked constantly, but never in the same spot. I'd dutifully place the pans around to catch the water, but it was necessary to move them because the leaks migrated. I learned to listen at night for the drip, drip that our visiting streams made.

I would deliver the bad news to Verl and he would promise that as soon as it stopped raining he would fix them. The ladder was never moved from its spot by the garage where he ascended with tar and determination "to fix the damned roof." He bought every new product for patching that came on the market and became an expert roof-fixer.

But it still leaked. The water had a way of running down the beams and dropping off wherever it pleased. I was constantly moving the pans along the floor under the beams trying to predict the landing of the next drip. It got particularly bad in the kitchen and dining area, dropping on the cabinet, counter and floor at will.

Of course I complained and my ingenious husband responded with his usual inventiveness. He stapled aluminum foil along one beam forming a shiny silver trough to catch the water that fell along it. At the end of this device he connected a plastic tube, secured to the foil with rubber bands and glue from a hot-glue gun. This tube carried the water to the kitchen sink.

The woman who cleaned for us thought he had stopped too soon. "Why didn't you have the tube go to the end of the counter where Florence has her plants. You'd have an automatic watering system."

I christened him, Mr. Rube Fixit.

Verl didn't think it was as funny as I did. I took pictures of his invention and showed it off to friends when we had a dinner party. It was there six months and it did do the job.

One summer Sunday, he decided to try a new roofing product and see if he could stop the leak in the kitchen once and for all. That day I sat out on the deck, spun wool on my spinning wheel and enjoyed the foothills and mountains on the horizon. These wonderful Sundays restored me and prepared me for the week ahead. Verl tramped back and forth on the roof, busy at his task, while I worked at mine.

I went into the kitchen to check the roast. I lifted the lid, it smelled wonderful, and I decided that we would have a nice dinner with wine out on the deck—romantic.

There was a loud crash and the roast and counters were showered with dust and wood splinters. I looked up and there was my husband sitting astride a beam, his work boots sending out little clouds of dust. The roof had given way under his weight. Although he was bruised by his sudden descent to the beam, it prevented him from falling ten feet to the kitchen floor. The hole in the ceiling was six feet in diameter and behind him I could see a hawk circling in the sky.

"Are you all right?" How often I asked that question!

"Yes, are you?"

"Yes." And then I began to laugh.

Verl looked down at me as though I was crazy, but then he smiled. My response was better than he might have predicted.

I picked the wood out of the roast and went to get the broom, dustpan and sweeper. Verl extricated himself from his perch, stepped carefully along the beams and climbed down the ladder. He went to get a roll of heavy-gauge plastic, the kind he uses to cover the greenhouses, the nurseryman's favorite material. He tacked it over the entire roof.

When the roast was done, I served it on the deck and drank three glasses of wine with dinner.

When Verl inspected the damage, he found that the insulation between the interior ceiling and the roof hadn't been ventilated properly. The wood sheeting on the roof had been kept wet and it rotted. The new roof cost more than the first house I owned—heavy plywood, treated to resist rot, new insulation and a newly developed roofing material.

Yes, you guessed it. The roof still leaks. Not as badly thank goodness. Still, when it frosts at night and then the sun comes out in the morning, we get drips in the bathrooms and kitchen. Verl says it is condensation and he must be right because it stops about noon. I have moved the best furniture away from under the beams because hard rains seem to bring leaks. Perhaps water gets into the beams outside and winds its merry, dripping way inside. The great new material that the roofer applied has curled up, blown off and been replaced by tar.

We are sort of philosophical about our problem roof. But if anyone asked, we'd say, "Never build a California house in Oregon."

# 6

## Water, Water, Everywhere

The valley where we live lies between the Cascade Mountain Range and the Coastal Range. The soil is deep and fertile and the Japanese Current brings warmth and moisture from the Pacific Ocean, just 50 miles west as the crow flies. From September until June it also brings rain, usually gentle, misty rain. But the summers are dry and the region is classed semi-arid desert during those months. In order for the plants we raise to grow, they must be irrigated.

Because of the mild temperatures, the micro-organisms that feed on the organic matter in the soil are active most of the year. They use up the organic matter which hold water in the soil and water must be added more often for plants to grow.

The aquifers that lie under the valley are deep, fed by the melting snow in the Cascades, so there is no problem with having enough water available. The only problem is getting the water pumped out of the ground and into the greenhouse, kitchen or shower.

On the two farms we have recently acquired, we have drilled irrigation wells. On the farm where we live, there are two irrigation wells and a well for the house. They are hooked up together in a system too complicated for anyone but Verl to understand. We have a close relationship with a man who drills wells and repairs pumps. Verl helped start the man and his wife in the nursery business.

Perhaps I should digress and tell a little about the nursery. It is a wholesale nursery, small compared to some of the giant businesses that employ thousands of people, but it is successful. Verl built his business by growing plants that are hard to propagate and are in demand. He grows very special blue spruce. One is called Hoopsi and is so silvery blue that it reflects light and glows pink at sunset. Another variety is perfectly symmetrical, bushy and slow growing. He discovered the mother plant as a chance seedling among a bed of thousands, recognized its unusual properties and began propagating it. He has cloned thousands of trees from the original tree and has patented it. He calls it Baby Blue Eyes. (Botanical names for conifers usually end in i.) He grows other ornamental evergreens, the kinds of trees that become the focal points of landscapes.

Kinnikinnick is a low-growing ground cover that is difficult to propagate. It is in the manzanita family and has small green leaves that stay green year round. In the summer, it has tiny pink flowers and in the fall, red berries. It tolerates drought and sun well and is sought after by landscapers who design public and highway projects. It is impossible to grow it from seed in a nursery. In the wild, the seeds pass through the intestinal tracts of birds and thus are prepared for propagation. (Did you ever wonder why the seeds you picked in the woods didn't grow?)

Since few nurseries are prepared to agitate seeds in sulfuric acid under prescribed conditions for 27 hours, it must be grown by cuttings. Verl developed the standard method of propagation. He was the first to inoculate the cuttings with spores of a fungus that grows naturally on the roots in the wild. This fungus increases the efficiency of the roots. Until this was known and added to the propagation method it was almost impossible to grow this plant in a nursery. We sell all we can produce and these plants are ready for sale in a year. Since the conifers might take as much as eight years to be ready to market, kinnikinnick provides a steady source of income.

Verl grows many varieties of deciduous trees, Japanese maples, beeches, etc., all of which must be propagated by grafting. He loves bamboo, which he says is his hobby plant, and he grows 45 varieties. Recently zoos have become our best customers for bamboo. Most of our plants are sold to retail nurseries in the Midwest and on the East Coast.

After this digression, we return to the subject of water.

All of the wells are powered by electrical pumps, so

if there is no electricity, there is no water. Verl does have a gasoline-powered generator and I suppose in a pinch for a few hours we could use that.

The greenhouses have various watering systems, depending on when they were built and what was the latest innovation displayed at the yearly trade show of nursery equipment. One large greenhouse has a traveling boom that, at programmed intervals, rolls down a 250-foot track, spewing a spray of life-giving water on the plants below. It works fine—until it gets off the track and drowns the plants beneath it in a deluge. When Verl is away, it is my job to worry about the traveling boom.

In another greenhouse, fifty or so small irrigation heads spit out a fine mist every fifteen minutes—when they are properly plugged in. The cuttings need to receive the proper amount of moisture from the air to sustain them until they develop their own roots and can draw it from the soil. If the sun heats the greenhouse and fries them too much, they die. If they are too wet, they rot.

When Verl is away, I have to watch the weather. If the sun emerges from behind the clouds, I rush to the main propagation house, study the tangle of electrical cords that are stapled to the ceiling and select the proper one to plug in. After plugging in three or four and lighting up the room or starting small motors, I find the right one and, whew, the cuttings are safe from drying and death.

The five acre "can yard," where plants grow in pots, is watered daily in summer, almost always in the evening when no one is working there. The cans are set on gravel so there is no mud under foot, but the unwary soul who traverses the yard is likely to get a shower. Recent environmental laws have ruled that there is to be no run-off from "can yards" and Verl is building a reservoir to collect, filter and recycle the water.

One night shortly after we were married, Verl, who sleeps nude, woke with a start. "Oh, my gosh, I left some water running. I'll have a flood."

He jumped out of bed, thrust his feet into a pair of rubber boots and dashed out into the night. We don't have any close neighbors and it was two in the morning, but I was still startled by his lack of apparel.

He was back in five minutes, chilled and wet. When he crawled back in bed he said, "No harm done. The plants are all right."

"Don't you think you should wear clothes when you go outside," the prude he sleeps with lectured. "A car might go by on the road."

"Gosh, dear, if I had worn clothes, they would be all wet."

End of argument. I warmed him up and we went back to sleep.

Verl once bought a computer to manage the irrigation. After a confusing month, in which the complicated instruction Verl described could not be correctly programmed, the computer and Verl gave up and he went back to the old system. The old system is the one in which an intelligent human must understand the following: The needs of the various plants, the vagaries of our three wells, Verl's Rube Goldberg electrical wiring, the relationship of sun and wind to temperatures in the greenhouses, and the principals of hydraulics. The human's job is to turn the proper switches and valves at the right times. Verl and several of our Mexican workers, who have had only a few years in school, possess this knowledge and skill.

One of my nightmares is that Verl would become ill, the employees who know the system would all go home to Mexico and I would become responsible for the watering. The scenario goes that I would fail and a million dollars worth of plants would dry up and die within a few hours. So much for bad dreams. Reality has been nightmare enough.

We were in the Portland Airport on our way to Europe when the following fiasco occurred. We didn't learn about it until we returned. Verl had hired a man with a portable sawmill to come and cut some cherry trees in our woods. What he hoped to do was have furniture made, perhaps a cradle, to give to our children from the fine old cherry wood. Besides, the trees at the edge of the field were taking water away from the trees Verl grew to sell.

The sawmill caught fire and the owner ran up to the nursery buildings to use the telephone to call the fire department. The truck came, tore down the lane, and ran over an aluminum irrigation pipe, forcing the water out the other end and flooding our neighbor's alfalfa field. The firemen continued on, unfurled a hose, sprayed water on the burning machinery and cracked the block. Thank goodness, no one paged us at the airport and we went happily on to Europe.

The damaged mill was in the back field for several months until the owner hauled it out without cutting the cherry trees. (The grandchildren arrived and survived without cherry wood cradles.)

Recently Verl hired a bulldozer and operator to level the land and dig the foundation for a new machine shed. He went away for a few minutes and the bulldozer operator decided to approach the site from a new direction. I was in the kitchen cooking and was washing my hands when the water sputtered and stopped.

I rushed out to find the bulldozer operator standing beside a newly created spring, scratching his head as he watched the water bubble out of the ground.

Verl arrived then and said, "Oh, the main line from the well is down under there." Then he laughed, "Say, that machine of yours is pretty heavy."

Not to worry, they shut off the pump, dug a hole, drained out the water and fixed the pipe. But I did worry. What would have happened if Verl hadn't been there?

We have mild winters here, usually, with only four or five nights when the temperature is below freezing. But once every three or four years it gets really cold— cold enough to freeze all those water pipes in the greenhouses. A few years ago, on one icy night, eighteen pipes burst. Verl treated this as a minor inconvenience and got out his plumbing tools to fix them. In fact he was much more concerned because the cold killed my favorite roses that night. I sometimes tease Mr. Rube Fixit, but I am more often grateful for my husband's manual talents.

The first ten years we were married I worked full time in Portland and most of our friends lived there. The 100-mile round-trip drive to see us didn't seem to deter them from visiting. One time I invited a new faculty member to come for dinner on a Sunday afternoon. I had been impressed by Joanne's abilities as a teacher and administrator. I was more impressed when she volunteered to play hostess at a tea to honor a visiting professor from Israel. Until that time the norm for entertaining at the school was Styrofoam cups, coffee from the cafeteria and silk flowers from someone's office.

Joanne must have felt the same revulsion to this casual style as I did. The tea she hosted was as elegant as any I have attended. She brought her silver tea service, beautiful linens and fresh flowers to the school to enhance the occasion. The faculty enjoyed this luxury so much, that tea set a new norm for entertaining. I decided that Joanne was a woman after my own heart and I wanted to know her better.

That Sunday I unearthed my grandmother's linen table cloth from the bottom of the linen drawer and pressed it. I brought in roses and carefully arranged the centerpiece, then set the table with my china, silver and the Waterford crystal that I seldom used. This was to be a special dinner for a guest who would appreciate my precious possessions.

The meal was almost ready. I peeled the potatoes and set them aside to begin cooking when Joanne arrived. While they simmered, we would talk and munch hors d'oeuvres. I stuck my head out the back door and called to Verl that it was time to shower. He was washing the Mercedes and said that he had to rinse it off and he'd be in in a few minutes.

I was in the shower, lathered with shampoo and soaped from head to toe when the water stopped. I waited long seconds for it to begin again thinking that the circuit breaker had blown and Verl would fix it. No luck. I wrapped a towel around myself and went to the back door.

"The water stopped."

Verl was holding a hose and looking at the soapy car. "I know. It must be the pump."

"How long till you fix it?" The faith of a country

wife!

"At least a half an hour."

"What am I going to do? I'm all soapy. Joanne will be here soon."

"You could use the water in the tank behind the toilet or go out to the irrigation well and turn the faucet on the side.," my helpful spouse replied.

Toilet tank water didn't appeal, so I walked out to the irrigation well. I was glad it was Sunday and no one but Verl would see me in the towel, hunched down by the faucet, which was a foot off the ground. I turned it on and freezing water gushed out. Verl says it is 55 degrees, summer or winter, but I swear it felt 33. By the time the shampoo was rinsed out, my head was numb. When the rest of me was soap free, I was blue with cold.

I dressed and greeted my guest. Then I took her out to the garage to meet my husband. Verl was standing in a foot of water, covered with grease and working on the pump with a huge wrench.

We ladies returned to the living room, munched hors d'oeuvres and talked. Joanne entertained me with tales of raising horses in Ohio and the vagaries of living on Guam. By the time the pump was fixed and Verl had disappeared into the shower, I finally put on the potatoes.

We toasted each other, being careful not to clink (and chip) the Waterford wine glasses, and became good friends, in spite of the late dinner and perverse pump.

Occasionally we meet people socially who tell us they love plants or flowers and dream of someday having a nursery. Sometimes they already have a little piece of land to serve as the beginning of turning their dreams into reality. Then Verl asks them how deep their well is and how many gallons a minute it will provide. If they blink uncomprehending eyes, I know that they have a lot to learn before they could be successful as nursery people. Knowledge and water are essential.

# 7

## *Oh, The Smell Of It*

Television commercials often portray the pristine nature of rural life. Green fields, trees and chirping birds are pictured and a blossoming cherry branch is held close up in front of the camera. As you watch, you can almost feel the breeze and smell fragrant fields and flowers—so different from the evil odors of the cities.

Yeah?

A mile west of our home, across two fields and a creek, is Flannery's Dairy. The name has been changed to protect the writer. This establishment was founded by a veterinarian and is run scientifically.

Fifteen hundred Holsteins stand in open air sheds all day and night. Since it seldom gets below freezing in Oregon, it is not necessary to have enclosed barns, and perhaps cows give more milk in the open air. All day these bossies engage in the scientifically monitored processes of ingestion, digestion, assimilation, excretion and lactation, all without moving more than a few feet. At prescribed times of the year the workmen, with shoulder-length rubber gloves, insert frozen semen into the cows' vaginas and that begins the process of procreation. The semen is obtain by fooling some poor desperate bull into fornicating with a dummy cow and then collecting the ejaculate. The resulting black and white calves are removed from the mothers and housed in doghouse-sized shelters, each with its own bucket. (This arrangement is reminiscent of the boxes that psychologist Skinner recommended for children.) The females are groomed to take their mothers' places and the little bulls are sold for meat.

So much for science. The smell of fifteen hundred times—you guess the number—daily loose cow plops wafting on the west wind is a rural experience you should avoid. But there is more.

The Flannerys collect the excreta of all those bossies, hold it in a lagoon and then periodically spray it on the fields. The crops grow and then are fed to the cows—scientific recycling at its best. The dairy has been cited by the Department of Environmental Quality for contaminating the stream that runs between the fields which divide us. The Flannerys pay their fines like good citizens.

This natural fertilizer is sprayed by an irrigation

boom. This device is a large pipe that sits vertically in the middle of the field. The pipe bends slightly at the top and rotates. A powerful pump pushes the liquid through the pipe and it sprays out on the field covering as much as ten acres as it turns. It looks like a huge angry snake spitting brown venom. Sometimes, however, the irrigation boom is placed too close to the road and, if the wind is blowing just right, passing cars receive a sprinkling of what we unscientifically term cow shit.

One day my husband was driving along the road in his blue Mercedes. The car is not new, but it is always shiny clean, and the personalized plates bearing his name announce to the world that the driver is no longer a poor little boy but a man who has made it. It was a pleasant day and the sun roof was open. The car ahead of him received a baptism of Flannery's natural fertilizer.

Verl's sympathies went out to the driver. In order to avoid a similar sprinkling he quickly turned off the road and drove into Flannery's field, crushing the young corn beneath his wheels. He made a wide circle in the field, avoiding the boom and spray, and left a wheel-print protest in the field before he drove back onto the road on the far side of the field. Several of Flannery's workers saw him detour into the field, but no one challenged him.

Sunday nights the Flannerys must flush their milk tanks. That is the night when the air is permeated with the odor of sour milk.

We have a large outdoor party most years, the Hardesty-Holden Hoedown, with a bluegrass band, square dancing and hay rides. When I plan the party, I always pray that it doesn't rain and that the wind doesn't blow from the west.

Incidentally, I never buy Flannery's milk.

On the east, adjoining our property, is a farm that until four years ago raised 4,000 hogs. Hogs smell worse than cows. Still, our neighbors raised them in an enclosed shed and the odor seldom reached as far as our house. Verl enjoyed passing by the hog operation when he drove the tractor hauling the hay wagon and our guests around the farm. It was fun giving our city friends a sniff of country life.

The hogs have gone. But in their place this year, we have a field of cauliflower grown for a frozen food company. The cauliflower has been harvested. They took only the heads and a few close leaves. The rest of the leaves and stems are left to rot in the field returning the nutrients to the soil. The resulting smell is such that if a person were bothered with flatulence and relieved himself of the gas that fomented in his intestines, nearby persons would think, "That damn cauliflower!"

Sometimes in the evening when Verl and I are in our bedroom sitting in our chairs in front of the television, I smell something. I sniff the air from the heat pump and wonder aloud about the origin. The smells that commonly swirl around our house do contain methane which smells like gas or electrical insulation burning. My husband dutifully hoists himself out of his leather cocoon and goes outside to sniff the air and bring me a verdict. Lately it has been Flannery's cows or the decaying cauliflower.

We live in a visually beautiful place. Sometimes it is beyond description. Every other year a company plants 90 acres of iris bulbs in the field beside our farm. In the late summer, the bulbs are dug up, the mature ones are sold and the younger ones are saved to be planted next year. The crop from that field is worth millions of dollars. In late May, when I look our from the living room or kitchen, the field is blanketed with blossoming iris, patches of purple, lavender, yellow, pink and even black. When the iris fields were in full bloom I always tried to entertain friends. I could offer them a view that most people dream about. Since we allow the iris nursery's workers to use our lane and eat lunch on our lawn, I can cut all I want and the house is filled with huge bouquets of iris and the fragrance of May.

We do have a few wonderful smells. In February and March the daphne in our yard blooms and the area is permeated with its scent. A few small blossoms, brought inside, fill the whole space with sweetness. In summers, many fields are planted with sugar beets which have a two year cycle. In Oregon, the seed is raised one year and harvested to be planted elsewhere the next year. When you drive past a sugar beet field, all you see are rows of ragged green plants. Then the smell hits you, and you drown in the rich fragrance, indescribably lovely, a blend of the marvelous scents of honeysuckle and clover honey. In those moments the smell of the country lives up to the television commercials.

If you come to visit us at times other than sugar beet or daphne blossoming, please be tolerant of the odors of rural life. And if you are very fastidious, carry a scented handkerchief.

# 8

## *Getting Ripped Off*

Verl's nursery is a wholesale operation. He says that he will sell to anyone who has the money, but only old friends or people referred from other nurseries come to buy one or two plants. Most of the orders come from the East Coast or Midwest retail nurseries or other wholesalers and are for hundreds or thousands of plants.

Verl has chosen to grow plants that are hard to propagate. He has become an expert at growing these plants and has built himself a niche in the market. When a landscaper gets plans from a landscape architect that call for kinnikinnick, one of our major crops, Verl's nursery is the one he calls. When it is a public project and bids are being made for the job, Verl will get calls from a dozen landscapers.

Verl loves his plants. Especially the beautiful blue spruce trees. Trees that are grown naturally from seeds are varied. Each one, like each one of our children, carries a different combination of genes that are expressed in slightly different characteristics. If you want a tree to be exactly like its parent, it must be cloned. This can be done in a laboratory by culturing the tissue from the plant. The variety of ferns that become house plants are propagated this way. Or, a piece can be snipped from the end of a branch and this cutting, with just the right moisture and care, may develop roots and become a little plant.

The most common method of producing a tree exactly like its parent is grafting. At just the right time of year—December or January for blue spruce—Verl cuts the ends from the branches of the blue spruce variety he wants to propagate. These cuttings are called scions. He brings the scions and ordinary field grown blue spruce seedlings to the propagation area.

Verl and the men he has trained sit under bright lights with very sharp knives. They carefully slice through the bark of the seedling, the understock, into the wood making a diagonal wound. Then they shape the scion with their knives to form a wedge that fits exactly into the slice. They must line up the cambium layers of the scion and the understock. The cambium is the living part of the tree, just under the bark, that transports the nutrients from the roots. The cambium performs in plants some of the same functions that blood vessels perform in animals. When the scion is exactly in place, they wrap the union tightly with a strip of rubber band.

The seedlings with their new branches are then placed in the greenhouse, where they are protected from stress and watered. The graft heals and, if the graft is well done, the scion becomes a living part of the seedling. Sometime after the seedling and scion begin to grow, the branches and top of the understock are cut away, leaving only the scion on the understock roots to grow and become a tree—a tree exactly like the one the scion was clipped from.

Verl grafts many of the trees himself and the employees who do the rest are his proud students. It is an activity that demands skill and care. Verl is able to graft very quickly, sometimes as many as five hundred trees in an eight-hour day. The employees have a good day if they can graft half that many. Verl's grafts take 97 percent of the time and the employees' results are about 75 percent. Many other nurseries have takes about 35 percent.

Once I asked him why he had more success in grafting than most people. He named a long list of variables that could account for it and then referred me to a doctoral dissertation that described the grafting of blue spruce at his nursery. Rather than read it, I concluded that Verl possesses a very green thumb.

When Verl had grown enough Baby Blue Eyes to market, he had it patented. This was a long expensive process involving attorneys, photographs and descriptions of similar trees . But it means that for 21 years, no one can propagate and grow this tree without paying Verl a fee.

The little trees are grown in a greenhouse for several years, potted into larger pots as they grow and then planted out in the fields. There they are staked, shaped, weeded, cultivated, fertilized and sprayed for pests. Finally, after as many as eight years of care, they are ready for market. Then they are hand dug, the root balls wrapped and tied with burlap, hauled out of the fields and carefully loaded on trucks. Verl always feels some sadness when they leave, as though he were sending children away from home.

Each of these trees represent years of hard work and care. To produce them payrolls must be met each week, workmen's compensation and hospitalization paid and gallons of water pumped. You can imagine how Verl feels when someone takes away his beautiful trees and then does not pay him. Yes, there are deadbeats even in the nursery business.

New customers pay cash. But as a cash-paying new customer becomes a regular, they ask for credit and it is extended. Recessions, bad management and unexpected bankruptcies occur and, ouch, there goes the money.

Verl has had particular trouble with Washington landscapers. Check-cashing laws in Washington are not as stringent as in Oregon and we have gotten bad checks—one for $6,000. The landscaper who bought from us put the nursery stock on a city project and was paid, but then his partner—his brother—absconded with the check. We have a lien on the house he lives in, but can't collect unless he sells the house.

Another painful experience occurred in Oregon. Verl grew 100,000 kinnikinnick plants on contract for a municipal project. The price was $100,000. He delivered the plants and they were planted. Then the landscape architect who ordered them said that they didn't meet specification and offered us $30,000. Verl knew the plants were the right size and he had other customers who would buy them, but they were already planted. While the lawyers negotiated, Verl consoled himself with fantasies about what he would do for revenge. The mildest dream was to go to the site in the middle of the night and spray them with herbicide. I didn't worry too much that he might do it because I knew he loved those plants and to destroy them would be against his nature. Finally a settlement was reached, for $66,000.

The City of Seattle wanted Oregon nurserymen to grow plants on contract to beautify public places. Rare plants were specified, not those that are usually on the market. A fresh young female horticulturist delivered the request to Verl as though she were presenting a lovely gift. Verl and other Oregon nurserymen who were approached smiled and said, "Thank you, but we can't help you."

Another Washington landscaping outfit ordered a large number of kinnikinnick to go on another government project. Verl said he would deliver them, but he would need half of the payment before he loaded his truck and the other half when he unloaded at the site. The check for the first half payment arrived. For some reason Verl took the check to his bank the day he got it.

The next day he loaded several thousand plants on his big yellow truck and took off for the five hour drive to a site near the Canadian border. When he got to the place, there was a lot of activity but no one available to help him unload. So he patiently took the plants off the truck, carrying two one-gallon pots in each of his large hands. Then he collected the check for the remainder of the payment and headed to the bank on which the check was written.

There was no money in the account. The check wouldn't clear. So back to the site went one mad nurseryman and reloaded his plants. The landscaper was at his elbow for the hour it took to do the job, pleading that Verl leave them or wait just a little while. No, Verl didn't hit him, he just concentrated on getting the plants back into the truck. Then he drove five hours back to Oregon, stopping only to refuel the truck with 50 gallons of gas.

That night at dinner I sat across from one frustrated man. Well, he sold the plants to someone else and marked the experience as a lesson expensive only in lost time.

Then, wonder of wonders, the first check cleared the bank. He called the landscaper but the phone was disconnected. A letter was returned and inquiries yielded the information that no one knew where the landscaper had gone. So Verl got paid for 1,000 kinnikinnick that he didn't sell. He marked that down as a plus on our side of the ledger.

# 9

## *More Rip Offs*

This scenario happens at least once a year. Verl loads his beloved plants carefully on a commercial truck and they go off to be delivered to customers in all parts of the country. The customers have contacted us through a broker. Both the broker and Verl guarantee that the plants are in excellent shape when they leave the nursery and will grow if handled properly. Usually, the truck has a number of stops to make before the entire load is delivered.

Several weeks later a call will come in or a letter will arrive. One customer says fewer plants than he ordered were delivered. Two of our people and the truck driver have counted the plants as they were loaded and all have signed the manifest that states the count was accurate. What happened and what to do?

If the trucking company and driver are known to Verl and the customer is one he has dealt with without difficulty in the past, he usually replaces the missing plants or charges less for the load. If he suspects the driver, he never uses him again. The broker also is concerned and may refuse to sell to nurseries who frequently charge that the count is short.

Verl sometimes gives a tree or two to drivers who admire them. They go happily down the road, anticipating planting them at their home in Montana, North Carolina or wherever they rest between long trips. Perhaps because they are doubly careful with the count when the truck is unloaded, there are fewer complaints when this is done.

Another drama that also occurs about once a year is the damaged product scam. Word will come through the broker that a new customer is complaining that the trees we delivered were smaller than the agreed-on size or that they were damaged or dead, etc. These nurseries are always 3,000 miles away or across the border in Canada.

The strange thing is that we will have sent thousands of trees out—same variety, dug at the same time and often in the same truck—and the other customers are jubilant about their purchase. And we have taken pictures of the fresh, beautiful trees as they were being loaded. Did the nursery mishandle them after they were delivered? Did the refrigeration on the truck die during the miles between stop one, where the trees were healthy, and stop two where they are saying they won't pay?

Once an Ohio nursery refused to pay. It happened to be near Cincinnati where my daughter and son-in-law live. While we were visiting there, Verl paid a call on the nursery posing as a prospective customer. There in the nursery yard were our trees looking beautiful with a price tag on them for five times the amount the owner was refusing to pay. Verl can tell his trees by the distinctive way he pins the burlap on the roots. He took pictures of the trees and, on the way out, gave the salesgirl his card telling her to give it to the owner. When we returned home, the disputed check was waiting. Both Verl and the broker crossed that nursery off their list.

One of our neighbors, a rhododendron grower, had an experience that is told in nursery circles with glee. The grower sent a semi, loaded with their beautiful rhododendrons, to a retail nursery on Long Island, New York. The sale had been arranged through a broker.

When the truck arrived, the nursery owner came outside and stood by the loading dock with a scowl on his face. The driver opened the back of the truck and the buyer peered in.

"These are not the prime rhododendron I ordered. They don't look like the pictures...Let's see, that one looks good, I'll take it and that one there." Then he turned to the driver and said, "Unload more so I can see which ones I want."

The driver said, "I need to make a phone call."

When he came back from the phone, he picked up the rhodies that were sitting on the dock, loaded them into the truck and closed the door.

"What's going on?" demanded the retail nurseryman, "I said I'd take those."

The truck driver was grim and silent. He started the rig, pulled out on the highway and headed down the road.

Five miles away he pulled into another retail nursery and was greeted by the delighted owner who had just received a call from a broker saying that a truckload of prime Oregon-grown rhododendrons had just become available and was on its way.

Several of our customers are former convicts who were Verl's students when he taught horticulture at Oregon Correctional Institution, a fancy name for a prison. They are now landscapers and doing well. They are among our favorite customers—no funny stuff with them.

# 10

## What's In A Name

When I married Verl, I kept the name Hardesty, the name I had taken 30 years before when I married my children's father. How easily at 20 I had given up my surname. As much as I cared for Verl, I could not imagine surrendering the label that had identified me for so long. I cringe at weddings when, after the ceremony, the minister introduces the couple to the congregation as Mr. and Mrs. John Jones. I feel that Mary Smith has just been obliterated.

Verl told the family and the neighbors that I was keeping my name for professional reasons. They were a little surprised, but accepted it expecting that I would become Mrs. Verl Holden socially. I didn't. I just couldn't.

There were other factors in this decision. I, too, had had a brief second marriage. It ended in three years without pain, only embarrassment that I could have made such a mistake. My second husband had been Zoltan, a Hungarian freedom fighter, younger than I, cultured and fun to be with. I suffered from my status as a divorcee and I am sure this clouded my judgement. The early Sixties were not as tolerant as today. I envisioned that this man and I would continue to have the good time we experienced while dating and that I would continue to manage the children. But after we were married, our cultural differences in regard to child raising became evident. Susan was at a difficult age and the situation with Zoltan became impossible.

During the time we were married, I completed a master's degree. I had taken Zoltan's name and the name on my diploma was an incomprehensible one, full of sz's and gy's. When we were divorced, I changed my name back to Hardesty, but my school records bore evidence of my mistake.

When I finished my doctorate and moved to upstate New York, I opened a private practice as a psychiatric nurse, doing marriage counseling and therapy. How could I display the diploma I had so proudly won when the name shouted my fallibility? I wrote to Western Reserve University and asked if I could have a new diploma. They replied that I could not. But they would issue a certificate that would look just like a diploma stating that I had received a diploma. I sent the fee with a sigh of relief and burned my original diploma vowing never to change my name again.

My younger daughter, Shevawn, was a teenager at the time and she watched this scenario. In addition, Shevawn admired a young colleague of mine who had graduated with her master's at 22 and who is known by every student nurse in the nation because she authored an excellent text book. The text, in its various editions had born three names as my friend's marital status changed. The author is again unmarried. Shevawn married George and is the mother of three little boys, but her name is still Hardesty.

Verl's nursery colleagues watch my determined feminism with some amusement. I feel respect and unspoken agreement from the women. Yet at the nursery association meeting when introductions are made, the man rises and says, "I am John Jones of J & S Nursery and this is my wife, Sally."

The sad part of this is that Sally has the degree in horticulture, inherited the business from her father and John is a stockbroker who dabbles in the business. The other introductions are the same.

Then Verl rises and says, "Verl Holden, Holden Wholesale Growers."

He sits and I rise. "Florence Hardesty, Holden Wholesale Growers." Then I sit.

Once I made a little speech about this and the women cheered, but nothing changed.

There have been a few mishaps because of our different names. We had the annual picnic for our chapter of the nursery association at our home for two years. I worked hard to make sure everything was perfect and was proud of my efforts. A card came from the secretary thanking Verl for his hospitality and apologizing for not sending thanks the year before. He was angry that I had been slighted. I decided to mention this omission to the secretary reasoning that, as a feminist, I should do my own complaining.

She apologized profusely and said, "I didn't know that Verl was married. He always came to the meetings alone."

I had attended every meeting with Verl.

The first year we were married, Verl would get phone calls that would go like this:

"Hello. Is Mr. Hardesty there?"

"No. There is no Mr. Hardesty here." Slam!

When I heard this, I said, "Honey, it might be important. What if I were in an accident?" Then I went on to explain that I replied to queries for Mrs. Holden with, "I am Verl's wife, Florence Hardesty."

After a few times he began to think it was funny. Especially when the caller insisted that he must be Doctor Hardesty.

We bought a house in Silverton to rent to our Mexican employees who had trouble finding a place to live. During the closing, when the papers were being filled out, the real estate agent said, "There, it's all taken care of, just as if you were married."

Friends stumble over my name in their nervousness, and one of my dearest friend never gets it right when she introduces me. I've tried to help her by giving her a clue. "Hard and dusty, just think of that and you'll remember."

Memorial Day came three weeks after we were married. We went to the cemetery where Alice is buried to put flowers on her grave. It seemed a little strange but I hope that if I were to die, Verl would do the same for me.

It was a bit of a shock to see that the gravestone was a double one with Verl's name and birthdate on the grave beside Alice's. "Together always" was carved into the stone. I've teased him about it and he has asked if I'd like him to buy some grave sites at the cemetery down the road from us. When I thought about it, I couldn't imagine being buried in an Oregon pioneer cemetery. I own graves in Pennsylvania where my parents and grandparents are buried.

The matter is unresolved. It is of no importance to me now. Perhaps such things are only important if you make them so—like what name I choose to be known by.

# 11

*Emerald Green*

Each year 13,000 trees are sent out from our nursery to all parts of the country. They must be dug by hand, the roots wrapped in burlap and firmly secured, and hauled out of the field. Then they are loaded on pallets to await the large trucks that will deliver them. If the order is a small one for a nursery in Oregon, Verl may deliver it in one of our trucks.

Digging can't begin until the trees are dormant. The soil must be just right, not too wet and not too dry. It can't be done when the ground is frozen. If spring comes early and the trees begin to bud, digging must stop. Finally there must be men to do the work. Digging properly, a necessity if the trees are to grow, is a highly skilled task. Our workers are very good at it, but they sometimes are slow to return from the trips they take to their homes in Mexico at Christmas.

All this results in a period of frantic activity from January until May. The trees must be ready when the buyers send their trucks.

Verl attempts to keep a close eye on the plants themselves, checking their foliage as he hurries by. Since we have three farms and he does so much of the hands-on work himself, it is hard for him to keep up with his inspections.

On one occasion he instructed the employees to dig a block of 50 arborvitaes and they did as he requested. However, when he inspected the trees, as they sat on the right side of the driveway at farm number two, he saw there was a problem.

Every tree had a six-inch circle of brown dead foliage near the base of the plant. He knew immediately what had caused it. We had had a warm fall, and warmth supports the proliferation of tiny, life-sucking red spiders. He had recognized the infestation and sprayed for it. (The pesticide clogs up the nasty little beasts' mouths so they can't suck.) Unfortunately the spiders had been active too long on the part of the plant which was warmest and had caused the needles to die.

Verl knew he couldn't send the plants out with a circle of brown on them, even though next year's growth would cover the brown spot. And, he knew the trees were healthy. He thought he might sell them to a

local landscaper who would understand the problem and be glad to get them at a discounted price.

Then he remembered a product he had picked up at the nursery supply store. It comes in spray cans and is popular in California. It covers brown foliage—Los Angelenos use it to paint their brown lawns green. This was a chance to experiment.

He sprayed the brown areas on the plants and they became a beautiful bright green, brighter even than the natural foliage of the plants which are called Emerald Green. So, not to be deterred, he sprayed the rest of the trees. They became, as he put it, "The damnedest, brightest green arborvitaes you ever saw."

"Oh, well," he thought, "We'll keep them watered and when they get their new growth, we will sell them."

He told his workers to dig 50 more from a part of the field unaffected by the mites and they did, lining them up on the left side of the driveway across from the super-green ones. Then he rushed off to another task.

The spring rush got more and more frantic. It was at the stage where I step aside if I find myself in the same hallway as Verl and allow him to rush past. One morning he took a load of trees to Portland. He instructed one of the new workers, a young blond man recently discharged from the Navy to load the other truck with the 50 arborvitaes on the left side of the driveway at farm number two. He planned to take it to a central location that afternoon where he and other nurseries would fill a truck with plants to go to New York. Then he headed down the road in his favorite *toy*, his own tractor-trailer with Holden Wholesale Growers painted in proud blue on the side.

He returned from Portland before noon and was given the message that the truck which would take the arborvitaes to New York was waiting to be loaded at another nursery. The workers said that his load was in the other truck so he hopped in and drove off.

When he got there, the long-distance driver was waiting impatiently for his load to be completed and there were Mexican laborers ready to help Verl transfer the load. Verl unlatched the back of the truck, pushed up the door and stared at 50 of the brightest green arborvitaes that had ever been seen. His new employee had loaded the painted trees from the right (wrong) side of the driveway.

Later he told me, "I was so mortified I wanted to crawl under them. I was just glad no one but the Mexicans and the truck driver were there to see those trees. "

He made a decision. He would send off the painted trees and then call the retail nursery in New York, explain, and offer a discount. So he hauled the 50 out of his truck and stacked them carefully in the box of the other truck.

That night in bed, he tossed restlessly.

"What's the matter, Honey?"

"That damn Jim put me in an embarrassing situation." Then he told me about the confusion. He was thinking of firing the employee who had caused him embarrassment. I pleaded that he give the fellow another chance. I have right and left-handed confusion and I was sympathetic.

The frantic pace of the spring season increased. Some days we had four trucks at the farm waiting to be loaded and often half the crew was out in the fields digging the order while the other half was loading the truck. In one instance, Verl climbed up into a truck bed to rearrange a load, which is a skill in itself. Pedro climbed up to help him, lost his balance and clutched on to Verl to keep from falling. They both fell and Verl pulled a hamstring. Being in pain and limping slowed him down only a little.

In May the hectic pace dropped off and there was hope that life could return to normal. I usually leave my study and go in to have lunch with Verl. When he comes in at noon, he brings in the mail, dumps it on the table, turns on the television to catch the news and the weather and then prepares his own hasty thousand-calorie lunch. He eats, reads his mail and answers the phone. (This is type A behaviour with a plus!) I fix my low-calorie lunch and read my mail while I get a flavor of what is going on in my husband's business.

This day he picked up an envelope and looked at the return address. "Oh, hell. It's from that nursery in New York—the one I sent the painted arborvitaes to. I forgot to call them." He tore open the envelope and a check fell out. "Well, they paid me."

Then he picked up the accompanying letter. "Listen to this. 'The arborvitaes were beautiful. We hope you can supply us with 1,500 next year.'"

He looked across at me, his green eyes twinkling. "Now what do I do? Do I paint them so they match the first 50?"

# 12

## Mexican Village

I live on the edge of a Mexican village in a rural area of Oregon that is commonly thought to be an enclave of Anglos. Verl, our American-born employees and I are the minority here. Fourteen, more or less, energetic dark-eyed people supply the major part of the work. When you wander into the propagation area, you hear Spanish music or the rapid exchange of conversation. When truck are being loaded, commands are exchanged in shot-gun Spanish, "Cuidado!",

"Alto!", "Aqui!" Small proud men sit atop large orange tractors and speed around the nursery dragging trailers loaded with dark green plants. In the fields, in winter, these compact powerful men work diligently and skillfully with their shovels, digging out trees without disturbing their roots so that when they are planted in yards in Massachusetts, or Illinois they will grow. In the propagation area three women do the monotonous work without complaint and six miraculous green thumbs result in hundreds of thousands of beautiful plants.

Three of our Mexican workers speak English well enough that they can communicate anything they wish. Of those, two have had three or four years of schooling and are embarrassed about their spelling and writing. The others range from knowing "Yes" and "No"— mostly yes with a smile—to having some idea of what is going on when English is being spoken. All are young. The 38-year-old man is considered aged.

In this chapter, I have changed the names of some of our workers to avoid embarrassing them.

What is it like not speaking the language of your village? I'll give you an example.

One Saturday morning, a blustery winter day, when the fields were a morass of mud, Verl said, "I'm going to take that truck load of nursery supplies down to your farm and unload the stuff in the barn. If the guys come to work, send them down to help me." Then off he went.

In half an hour I heard the sound of Jose's souped-up car and knew the men had come to work. So I went out and called, "Buenos dias!"

They approached me smiling.

I delivered Verl's message slowly in Spanish,

enunciating clearly. (I had worked on the two sentences with the help of my Spanish dictionary.) Then I said, "Comprende?"

The smiles were broad and the eyes bright. "Si, Si, Senora."

At noon Verl came home for lunch.

"Did the guys find you?" I asked.

"No, I unloaded the whole damn truck by myself."

That evening he told me that they had spent the morning wading around in the muddy field trying to dig trees.

I am now in the middle of my second year of Spanish at the community college. Verl, who had six weeks of Spanish in the seventh grade, is learning from the employees. I keep buying him learning aids, like a credit card-sized computer that translates—the damn thing is too small to be practical—and tapes. I can take a simple message when the phone calls from Mexico come and no employees are here. Verl has learned how to give directions in Spanish. And now I could tell the men, *"Verl dice: ustedes van al otra ranco y lo ayudan a Verl."* ("Verl said: you go to the other farm and help him.")

Where did the stereotype of the lazy Mexican come from? I have never met such energetic, hard-working people. They will work six or seven days, if we need them, and as many hours as necessary.

Once Verl said, "Gosh, Ernesto, I hate to ask you fellows to work ten hours but we have to get this order out."

Ernesto said, "This is better than working for my father. He made us work twelve hours, seven days of the week and no pay."

More than half our workers are Ernesto's brothers,

nephews or cousins. Perhaps we should thank Papa Santos for the excellent output of our nursery.

One night Verl heard a truck drive into the nursery. When no one came to the door, he went out to investigate, carrying a shotgun. When he approached a parked pick-up, a frightened Ernesto sat up on the seat and said, "It's me! Don't shoot!"

He went on to say that his wife, an American woman, had kicked him out and he had no place to go. He moved into Verl's office and camped out on the couch.

Six of his relatives, also our employees, had been sleeping in Ernesto's garage. The next day they were also homeless and scattered around the county, moving into labor camps with friends. It was impossible for them to find a house or an apartment to rent.

Verl and I began immediately to look for housing for them. The men asked if they could move into my barn which was then adequate only for our sheep. We said, "Wait. We'll find you something."

We found a small house in the nearby town not far from the high school, and bought it. We rent it to them for less than the standard rate. At first I was concerned that with six men living there they would be crowded. So we enclosed the front and back porch—and six more moved in. Some are our workers. Others are their fathers, brothers or "cousins visiting from California."

I have stopped worrying and keep telling myself that it does look like the men's dormitory of the college. They have two television sets and cable service so they can watch the Spanish station. They asked for another refrigerator in order to buy food in bulk. Their housekeeping is about what you would expect from 12 men. It is better when Ernesto, the crew chief, is there. They do keep the lawn mowed and watered and pick up the debris the high school kids toss about carelessly.

When we try to find out how many people are living there, we get vague answers. Most of the men spend two months in Mexico so their beds are empty. Others have moved on to better jobs and have begged to stay and Verl has assented. A fellow who worked for us for a week several years ago, then hurt his back, lived there without working for a long time. We think he kept house.

At the first of the month, Verl's wallet bulges with small bills. Each man pays his share of the rent, water bill, gas and electricity. They had no phone so they used our nursery phone. When Verl got the phone bill, he marked the phone calls to Mexico and California and posted it. The men looked at it and then paid what they owed him in small bills and change.

This was inconvenient. So Verl signed for them to get a phone at the house where they live. All was well until the month when the bill was $500, including one $200 call. Since Verl is ultimately responsible for the bill, he had the phone company put a stop to all long-distance calls. Negotiations between Verl and the men are occurring about how the bill will be paid and what will be done to prevent huge bills in the future. This situations resembles ones I helped to solve when I taught in a small college. The language is different, but phone problems exist when young people are far from home.

Our workers have a problem other than large phone bills and not speaking English. They are unfamiliar with machinery. Lessons that our grade school children, especially boys, learn by listening to their parents talk about automobiles and using the power mower are not part of the experience of men who grew up in an isolated Mexican village. As much as they love to drive the big tractors, if one stops running, they are prone to dismount and leave it in the field. Most often they neglect to turn off the key and don't tell anyone there is a problem. One of our employees is a mechanic who finds the poor machine, recharges the battery and solves the problem—usually by replenishing the gas tank. Verl tells me that is why he has to have fifteen tractors.

Paradoxically, they love cars. It was José's proudest day when he became the owner of a lipstick-red Camero. He barrelled into the driveway of the nursery and the other men stood in an admiring circle inspecting his wheels.

But in a week, José had a problem. The police had stopped him and on finding he had no driver's license or insurance, impounded his precious car. To add insult to injury, they charged him $10 a day for rent. Poor José was making $5 an hour.

Verl came to the rescue. He purchased the car from José for several dollars, got it out of jail and stored it in our machine shed. José could visit it at lunch time, but Verl had the keys. Then José studied the driver's manual, learned how to park and paid his fine. Finally he passed the driver's test, bought back the car and got car insurance. Now he doesn't roar in with the old dash, but he is legal.

The roster of our employees changes since the men go home for long vacations or to solve a crisis on the farm in Mexico. But they come back sometimes in a few month, others in a year or two. Frequently, we have only one man who is licensed to drive. Verl assigns the van to him and he becomes the transportation manager driving the men to their house. Ernesto and a man who is married to an American woman help the rest with problems such as filing their income taxes.

When they need help, we come to the rescue. Oswaldo was arrested for shoplifting an a local discount store. He had bought a hat several months before and now he was accused of stealing it. The band inside the hat was sweat stained and even the policeman was reluctant to arrest him. But the store insisted. Verl got instructions from our lawyer and accompanied our frightened employee to court. Fortunately, the store dropped the charges. Another worker was named by a woman he had never met as the father of her child. The worker's wages were going to be garnisheed for child support. Verl and the lawyer straightened that out.

When the men go to Mexico, they leave everything there, a new pick-up, their clothes and all their money. Two or three weeks after they have promised to return, frantic collect calls from Mexico are received. Verl sends money orders and in a week or so we get a call to pick them up at the bus station or airport. And then these faithful sons and husbands return to work with a debt to repay, families to support in Mexico, and the need to save money for the next year's trip home.

The three women who work for Verl are from another family. Two are sisters and the third is their cousin. They are intelligent, ambitious women who handle the propagation for the nursery with ease. Isidra, who speaks English, has management potential as well. But when I suggested that she and I take a class to prepare us for the certified nursery exam, she said, "I write and read English like a second grader."

I dropped the idea that she should become a certified nurseryman and attended workshops to become an English tutor. Now I am teaching Isidra to read and spell. The other two women are my English students. Classes are held at noon three days a week in the propagation area. We began by teaching Olivia the words she will need to explain to the doctor when her labor pains begin.

I met Carmen, Isidra's daughter, last spring. Carmen became ill at school and her mother went to get her. The earliest doctor's appointment that could be made was in the late afternoon. So Isidra returned to work and settled Carmen in her car with blankets and books. When I learned that she was there, I brought her into the house. Carmen and I became instant friends.

She is the best behaved eight-year-old I have ever met. The only other girl who possibly compares with her is my granddaughter, Leslie. Carmen could teach Leslie a lot about manners and I wish Carmen could have a few of the educational advantages that Leslie enjoys.

When school vacation came, Carmen began coming to work with her mother. We played in my pool and I taught her to swim. When Carmen noticed Leslie's letters attached to the refrigerator door, she began to write me letters and stories. With my grandchildren so far away, Carmen fills a void in my life. I hope that I do the same for her.

I want to be a part of this Mexican village that I live in, but there are barriers. The language is only one. There are social and cultural differences as well. But there is also affection. And if I study my Spanish and am patient, I will become more than the *Patrona*.

# 13

## Relatives

When Verl and I married we acquired each other's relatives. I got the best of the arrangement in that I got more. My daughters were grown, out of college and had established careers in the east. Susan had married Jim, and Shevawn and George were constant companions. We had agreed when we made our verbal marriage contract that I could always visit my children and he would never object. I do visit, three or four times a year and every other Christmas. Verl had chosen to come with me once a year. Now there are grandchildren and when Grandma arrives without chosen to come with me once a year. Now there are grandchildren and when Grandma arrives without Grandpa Verl, I hear, "Where is Grandpa Verl? Why didn't he come too?" I suspect he will be visiting more often.

Verl's children had experienced three difficult years by the time we were married. Adjusting to a new stepmother was just one more hurdle. Kristi, at 14 when Alice died, had been rebelling. She was engaged in a typical teenage struggle with her mother who seemed so competent that Kristi could never hope to emulate her. Kristi later told me that Alice's death seemed to be the ultimate weapon against her. How could she become independent when her mother whom she was attempting to leave, suddenly was gone? Verl, too, was struggling to cope with his loss. How would he manage the children? Kristi continued to rebel and Paul seemed too grown up. The demands of the nursery continued while Verl struggled with the income tax forms, the kid's homework and preparing meals. He tried to enlist Kristi as cook, but that led to more conflict. He was desperate to find someone to help him.

Some cousins introduced him to a recently divorced woman with two teenaged children. Betty was lively and fun to be with. They married ten months after Alice died. Betty's daughter moved into Kristi's room with her and the family room was converted into a room for Betty's son. It soon became apparent that the marriage had been a mistake. Verl had exchanged one set of problems for another. The children formed battle lines. Betty wasn't a relaxing companion when they were at home, and Verl was still mourning Alice. Betty viewed this as a personal affront and removed all traces of Alice from the house.

After ten months, Verl and Betty decided to end the marriage. He backed one of his trucks up to the house, removed Betty's furniture and took it to her brother's house. Then Verl, Paul and Kristi returned to the task of completing their mourning and adjusting to life without Alice. By the time I entered the picture, the three Holdens were managing rather well.

Kristi was amused by her father's dating. It had become a family game to evaluate each new woman he invited for dinner at the house. Kristi dissected each lady with cutting wit. Once I asked her about a woman Verl had dated. She replied, "Think of a walnut. Now put a bouffant hairdo on it." I never learned how I had been classified. Paul wasn't much interested in his father's women friends. He pursued his own interests— sports, television, and eating when and what he liked. He had learned not to bother grown-ups. I was just another of his father's friends. Verl's children rather liked me, but didn't expect that I would be around long.

I had read all the books about step-parenting and had seen plenty of bad examples from my marital counseling practice. Considering Paul and Kristi's ages and their history, I knew that I could never become a mother to them. Still, I would be their father's wife and I hoped eventually to become a special friend.

Verl made the major decisions about the children and if they needed to be disciplined he did it. I offered advice openly, but I made sure it was always clear that it was only advice and that I would support fully any decision he made. I advocated for the children if I felt it was warranted, but I made sure everyone knew that I was an advocate without power. I became the mistress of the house, with Verl's full support, and the children were to respect that. What they did in their rooms was their own business unless it jeopardized the household. Kristi had some trouble with this last rule and most of our early conflicts were territorial. The plan worked in that the children have not interfered with our marriage. Perhaps I might have become more to the children if I had involved myself to a greater extent in their upbringing.

Kristi is a vivid brunette with large dark eyes and wild, naturally curly hair. Until curly hair became fashionable, she spent hours in front of the mirror, burning out scores of dryers, trying to straighten her beautiful hair. Kristi is wonderfully witty with an uncanny ability to recognize the ridiculous. She is determined not to be ordinary, even when ordinary is logical and comfortable. For a time it seemed as though she was going through life looking for things to stumble over. Deep in her core she has the same values that her mother and grandparents had: honesty, frugality and independence. Her life has been exciting and yet hard.

She left for college four months after Verl and I were married. Although she has only been at home a year all told during our marriage, we have managed to have a score of rip-roaring, yelling, tearful fights. And yet I am her trusted confidante. We do love each other, and we have learned to respect the other's territory and roles. She is now thirty and has completed a degree in journalism. She has lived in Eugene, seventy miles away, and in Boston—with and near my daughter, Shevawn. She now lives in Portland. Eventually she will find her life's work, something that will use her fine mind, creativity and quirky sense of humor.

Paul is a careful young man. He has always been polite and thoughtful with me, but a trifle remote.

There have been a few wonderful open times. At his eighth-grade graduation, when the students presented a rose to their mothers, he came into the audience where I sat with his grandmother, kissed me and gave me his rose. I had been his stepmother two weeks and I was moved to tears. In high school, he sang the lead in *Carousel*. I went every night and used a pocketful of Kleenexes. But these moments have been the exception. At fourteen, he was his own man and not about to allow an interloper to set rules for him. I tried and when it didn't work, I arranged things so that my requests were met. (Okay, so that's manipulation.) For example, he likes to eat in the living room in front of the television. My oriental rug and tapestry couch were suffering. I instituted a "No eating in the living room" rule, but it was ignored. I moved one TV into our large bedroom and the other into his room. The meal-time garbage moved into Paul's room and that was the end of that problem. But we spent our evenings apart and missed the opportunity to become closer.

I wanted him to become responsible for maintaining his clothes. My daughters had always done this, at a much earlier age, and Kristi managed her clothes—one piece in the washing machine at a time. I didn't mean to be punitive, I just thought everyone should know how to take care of his own clothes. Paul refused. I waited, thinking that necessity would drive him to comply. But his grandmother intervened, in spite of his father's and grandfather's protests, and took it upon herself to do Paul's laundry. I withdrew in defeat. Grandma said that it gave her a chance to see Paul when he picked up his newly ironed clothes at her house. Later, I had a malicious chuckle when Paul found a female roommate and, although he was close by, Grandma didn't receive a visit for a year. He had found someone else to wash his dirty clothes. (I am happy to report that he now visits his grandmother regularly. I can't be malicious very long.)

This year Paul married a lovely young woman, Julie. The remoteness is gone and he is closer to both Verl and me. He is doing well at his work and I hope that someday he will choose to return to the nursery and run it.

I acquired another relative when I married Verl—a ghostly one. I moved into the world and place that had been occupied by Alice. Betty had attempted an exorcism. She had redecorated the house, removed all of Alice's belongings and made certain that no pictures of her remained on display.

I was shocked when I realized this and immediately asked to see Alice's picture. Verl brought it out from where it was hidden and I put it on the mantel in the bedroom. Their wedding presents had been packed in a cedar chest and moved to Alice's parent's home, awaiting the time when Kristi would have her own home and could use them. I asked that the chest be brought back and placed in Kristi's room so that she could enjoy them.

Betty hadn't removed the hundred jars of fruit and pickles that Alice had canned. It seemed to me that what Alice had produced was much more personal than the wedding presents, most of which had never been used. I tried to serve them to the family, but the children didn't like canned fruit or pickles. This seemed so sad. Their mother had worked to prepare food for them and they were determined to waste it.

I learned to know Alice through the memories of the people whose lives she touched. They told of a bright, honest, strong woman, full of fun and jokes. She developed rheumatoid arthritis shortly after she and Verl were married. She was chronically ill for many years. In spite of pain, fatigue, and thirty surgeries to reconstruct her hands, she led a productive life. She was active in the community and used her accounting skills to manage the business part of the nursery. I attribute the firm financial basis of Verl's business to her good judgement.

In my family, china and silver are the prized possessions of the woman. The Baird and Marshall women treasure their pretty things and I entered the marriage with a truck load. When Verl was in the Air Force in Japan, engaged to his college sweetheart, he chose a gift for her, a set of lovely china, white with one large pink rose in the center of each plate. Alice had never used it. She was always saving it for a special time. Then in her early forties she died.

I leave my china in the cupboard and use Alice's when I have her relatives here for the holidays, or for parties where her sorority sisters are guests. I always think of her when I set the table and arrange a centerpiece of roses. I'm sure that if she is somewhere and knows what I am doing, she approves.

Verl's mother and brother live three miles from us. His father died last year at 84. His parents had moved from Salem to be near Verl when Alice died, wanting to help. Although they put some prenuptial pressure on Verl to choose a more suitable woman, I have had no difficulty with them since we've been married. Verl's father worked for him until he was 80. An intelligent, self-educated, hardworking man, there was a special spark of affection between us. Verl's mother has a hard time understanding me, her life has been so different from mine. Perhaps this lack of understanding is mutual. But we do care a great deal for each other.

Verl's sister, Pat, is a talented, sophisticated lady. She married a career army officer who was Verl's fraternity brother. They moved to Portland when her husband retired shortly before Verl and I were married. We enjoy and appreciate each other and much of our social life is spent together. Verl and Pat have a special, close relationship and I enjoy observing them.

Verl's brother, Larry, has been chronically mentally ill for the last twenty years. He lives with his mother. He is a nice man, a good person who has been prevented from living a full life by his illness. At first, his parents ignored the suggestions I made about how they should respond to Larry, discounting the fact that I was teaching graduate nursing students and psychiatric residents the same skills. Then one Saturday, Pat called and said the folks were having a terrible time managing Larry. I went over and stepped into a volatile situation. Larry was shouting and livid with anger. He was sure his room was bugged and the folks would not give him $2,000 to have it debugged. I talked with him and persuaded him to take his medicine. In a few minutes, the crisis had passed.

For the next four years, I was in contact with Larry's psychiatrist and helped Larry manage his medication. During this time, he had a volunteer job, taking care of an irascible, brain-damaged old gentleman. The person with the longest tenure in that position, before Larry, had lasted two weeks.

After Verl's father died, the relation between Verl's mother, Larry and I shifted. Suddenly, as far as the medication or advice went, I was the "bad guy," with Larry and Mom allied against me. My family therapist colleagues confirmed my theory that I had become part of a triangle that met some of Mother's and Larry's unconscious needs. I suspect that I had assumed the role as "bad guy" that Dad had occupied until he died. Larry refused to follow the medication regime and the psychiatrist refused to treat him any longer. Someone threw his medicine down the toilet and I resigned my role as consultant.

Larry found a new doctor and together they resumed responsibility for his medications. Mother says he is, "Fine." Although he is no longer volunteering, that seems to be accurate. For many years, Larry was viewed by other members of the family as Mother's burden. Now he is the person who is her major companion and his presence enables her to continue living in her home.

Alice's parents introduce Verl as their son and that describes the relationship. It continued after we married. All the holidays and birthdays were spent at the Knox's or with them as our guests. Alice's parents were successful farmers and in many ways they were more like my grandparents and relatives than the Holdens. I especially like Uncle Glen, the younger brother (80 years old) who lived with the parents. (At one time, six brothers had lived on the farm.) There were times at the Knox's I can only describe as weird. I heard all about Alice, her college career and her wedding. I was shown the pictures and the dress. At dinner there would be reminiscing about old times. I had no jealousy—after all, Verl and I each had a life before we met. But how was I to respond? I comforted Clara when she told me about losing her oldest daughter, and did my best not to damage the bonds between the Knoxes and Kristi, Paul and Verl.

Alice's younger sister, Doris, was widowed about the same time that Alice died. Doris's Aunt Nancy had a great idea. If Verl and Doris would marry four children would have parents and the Knox inheritance would be consolidated. Doris's teen-aged daughters were crazy about Verl and thought that this was a great idea. Verl had one date with Doris, but couldn't shake the feeling that he was dating his little sister. I suspect that she had the same response.

I knew about Aunt Nancy's suggestion. One time at a family dinner, a month after we were married, Aunt Nancy took me aside and whispered, "Florence, when are you are going to have your baby?"

I laughed and said, "I'm not pregnant, I'm just plump." I was past fifty at the time.

I decided that Aunt Nancy meant no harm. But for several years I did feel a little strange about Doris.

I had an extra set of in-laws for almost ten years. Logistics of the holiday celebration were sometimes cumbersome. The Knoxes lived more than an hour away over winding country roads and were in failing health. As time passed, I became very fond of Alice's family. Then one by one, the old people died. Verl and Doris planned the funerals and I felt a real sense of loss.

Paul and Kristi inherited a small nest egg, which made their life easier, and there was also some bank stock for Verl. He bought me a mink coat from part of it. Perhaps that was a coincidence, but I like to think it was a thank-you.

At first, I thought the bond to the Knoxes were severed. But when the holidays came, the prospect of celebration without Doris and her daughters was unthinkable.

I am so much richer because Verl's family has become mine.

# 14

## Cleaning Ladies

In my role as teacher, counselor and mother, I have advised many young women to hire a cleaning person. This advice is given following a recital about how tired the woman is after work or school and how difficult it is to get their husbands to take responsibility for household tasks.

My advice is usually greeted with discomfort. I've heard things like, "I don't want anyone else in my house," or "I'd feel strange having someone clean up after me," or "I wouldn't know how to act with them."

Incidentally, most husbands I've talked to think that having a cleaning lady is a great idea.

The responses of the women reflect the attitudes of middle-class Americans who haven't had any experience with servants. Now, I haven't had servants either, but I have hired people to help me and helpers were not foreign to my family.

My grandmother had a hired girl, a young neighbor woman who helped her do the woman's share of the farm work. During the Depression, when my mother was employed by the WPA, we had a cleaning woman, a powerful Russian woman who wore out baskets of cleaning cloths with her scrubbing. Mother bartered English lessons for this service and helped Olga become a citizen. After I was divorced, I needed a baby-sitter for my children. There were no day-care centers in those days. I found a wonderful woman, Willie Mae Davis, who became a second mother to my girls, and a good friend. Willie Mae and I had trouble finding ways to address each other that were comfortable. I could not call her Willie Mae as long as she called me Mrs. Hardesty. She seemed embarrassed when I used Mrs. Davis. Time passed and we adopted the children's names for us. She became Baby-sitter and I became Mommy.

When I did my own cleaning, I would experience a pleasant feeling of righteousness. I would stand and survey my handiwork, sniff the odor of soap and polish, and admire the order I had created. I was delighted to find that when I came home from work on the day the cleaning woman had been there and smelled the smells and admired the order, I felt the same righteous satisfaction. I would pay the cleaner with the money I had earned at the hospital and have enough left over to pay the woman who typed my papers.

When I met Verl and visited his home, I was upset by the low standards of cleanliness that existed. (Euphemism for the place was a mess.) Verl dashed through the house once a week or so with the sweeper if the work at the nursery permitted. For a while before we were married, I avoided invitations for meals at his home. I finally told him that I wouldn't eat there unless he hired someone to clean the kitchen.

The idea had never occurred to him. He found two women who were earning money for their fundamentalist church. They took pity on this poor widower with his motherless children and attacked the disorder in the house with religious fervor. They cleaned the cupboards and drawers, the freezer and the refrigerator, and washed walls and windows.

Verl was amazed. He said, "I thought you had to get married to get these things done for you. I didn't know you could hire it."

When we married and I appeared in the household, some of their ardor for cleanliness vanished. The ladies weren't saving the poor widower any longer. They found other jobs and we had a long succession of people to clean for us.

Most of the women had been housewives. They had little training for a job, but wanted to work. This job served as a transition between working in their own homes and higher-paying jobs. One woman was trained as a teacher and had let her teaching certificate lapse. She worked at cleaning to pay for the university courses she needed. We were happy when she was hired as a teacher, but sad to lose her services.

Alma was a woman in her late thirties with six children ranging in age from 10 to 20. She brought one or two of her family with her and assigned chores. On occasion a grandchild would also arrive in the van crowded with the mops and pails. Their work was good but I worried about my Waterford crystal and Royal Copenhagen figurines when this crew arrived. I solved that problem by buying a glass display case and moving my most fragile possessions into it.

For a while we had a professional cleaning service. I loved them. A team of four women arrived. The owner would commandeer the kitchen and direct the others in their specialized tasks. An hour later they would leave a shining house. But they cost twice as much as the other people we had employed and since Verl paid for the weekly cleaning (my contribution was the daily chores), I was overruled and we stopped using the service.

Currently our cleaner, Julie is an attractive redheaded widow about forty. She drives up in her sports car with her mops and buckets beside her. She receives a federal pension and owns several homes and a beachfront cottage. She is a licensed beautician and has held secretarial jobs, but she likes the freedom and physical work that this job offers. Once she put an ad in a singles' column and received a deluge of replies. But Julie is discriminating and it may be a while before the perfect man arrives and insists that she retire.

Mary Ann cleaned for us for several years. She is a woman in her late thirties who lives on a small farm in the foothills of the Cascades. One day we were chatting about pets and she told me the sad tale about the demise of her favorite pet, Daisy.

When Daisy was a little pig, her mother laid on her.

Mary Ann rescued the infant porker and moved her into the house. The children bottle fed the baby and she grew. She learned to eliminate on newspaper in the corner of the family room and was in every way a clean and pleasant house pet, begging scraps from the table and watching television with the children. Daisy slept near the wood stove and would move closer as the fire burned low.

Time passed and soon Daisy weighed 250 pounds. When she attempted to cuddle the stove, she moved it. Mary Ann's husband was afraid she'd start a fire. In spite of pleas from his wife and the tears of the children, this family member was moved to the pig pen in the back yard.

Daisy was very unhappy. She escaped several times, pushed open the door and returned to the warmth of the hearth. It is hard to argue with a pet that size.

One winter morning a neighbor, an elderly bachelor, came down his stairs to begin the day and discovered his front door wide open. There by his wood stove was Daisy, snoring happily. The irate farmer called Mary Ann's husband who arrived in his truck and took Daisy straight to the slaughterhouse.

When Mary Ann finished telling me this story her face was wet with tears and while a part of me was sympathetic, the rest of me was stifling an impulse to laugh.

Every time I hear someone say, "My house is like a pig pen," I think of Mary Ann and her pet pig, Daisy.

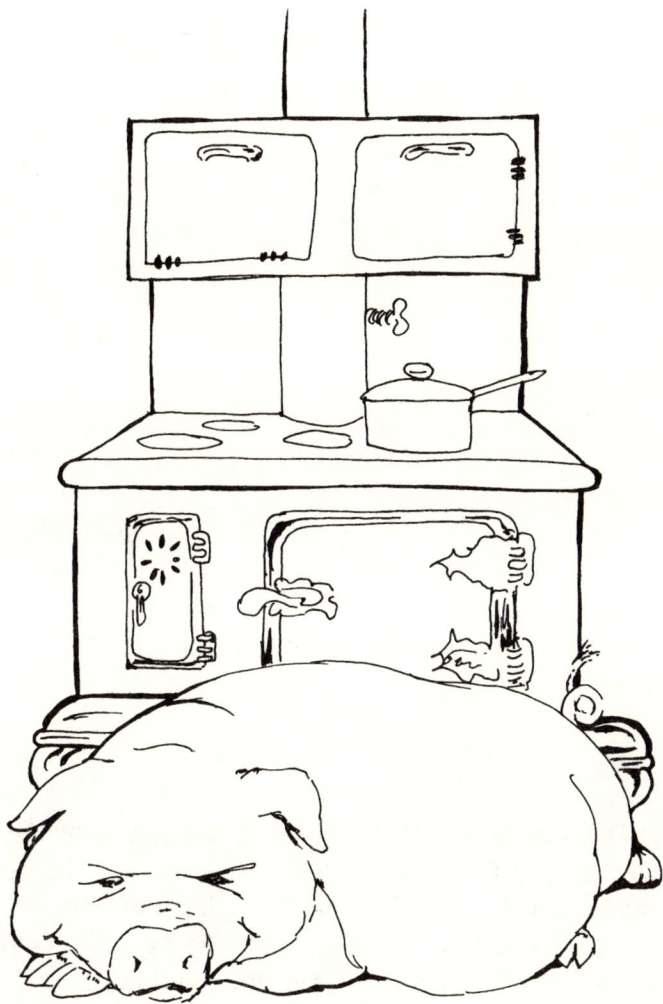

# 15

## *Summer Solstice*

One day last June, I was unaccountably nostalgic, something difficult to understand on such a lovely summer day. I began checking through my mind for the reason, a practice I had encouraged my clients to follow. Then it came to me. The day was June 21st, the day that, 44 years before, gownd in white lace, I had become a bride.

It was so romantic in those days. The boys came home from the service and we marched off to the altar in pairs, living all the dreams that had sustained us when the men were in Europe or the South Pacific.

I hadn't known my first husband well. I thought I did, since we had *gone together* for four years. However, we had been apart most of the time. He was my brother's friend and I started to date him at the end of May when I was 16. He was tall and blond and looked as though he owned the world. He had passed the test to become a naval officer and was to leave July first. We whirled through the month, sitting up on the front porch until very late and taking long walks. By the time he left, we were promised to each other.

A year later I began nursing school. I wanted to contribute to the war effort. Also, nursing would be a good preparation for marriage, which then meant babies and a house. I wrote to him every day and he answered whenever he could. The war ended and he came home. I was 300 miles away in school so the letters continued. We crammed in weekends in Philadelphia where the only place we could be alone together was the cemetery near the school.

I had doubts but I fought them down. Other men were interested in me, attractive men with whom I had more in common. But they frightened me, so I clung closer to my dream man and married him on a beautiful June evening.

I had become a wife without the testing that a normal courtship entails. Our relationship was formed in a situation where each of us had the opportunity to present ourselves in the best light. Strong sexual attraction, held in check by the fears of pregnancy, clouded our appraisals of each other.

It all ended 12 years later when I took my young daughters and left him. He married his secretary as soon as the divorce was final. They are still married, have raised a family and seem happy.

I was distressed to realize that this anniversary made me sad. I've had a good life, full of adventure and a successful career and now I have a happy marriage. My daughters are lovely women and good mothers.

I mentioned the date to my daughters when I made my weekly phone call. Each said that they liked the way they had grown up and that they were always struck by how different I was from their father. Then they went on to talk of important things, like the grandchildren and their jobs.

That evening I told my husband the things I had been feeling. He told me about his courtship and marriage. He had married two weeks after he returned from two years of military duty in Japan and his courtship had been much the same as mine. We talked about the era, the pairing off that occurred, the pressures to marry and the expectation that most of one's fulfillment would result from marriage. He felt that he had been lucky in that he and Alice were well suited and both were committed to maintain the marriage. They had been together 20 years before she died.

We laughed over each other's stories and cried a little about lost dreams. There was no jealousy about the past or recriminations, only interest and acceptance.

After a little while I concluded that the summer of life is for the young. The best time is now—in the fall.

# 16

## The Great Raspberry Caper

I was busy that summer day when Verl came in for lunch. I was entertaining my Spanish class at four and was hurrying to get things ready. I smelled Verl before I saw him, a familiar fragrant odor. When he came into the kitchen, the first thing I saw was that his blue shirt bore rose-colored polka dots.

"Raspberries?"

"Yes, look at my hands." They were stained deep pink. "Come out to the lunch room and see what we've got."

I followed him to the trailer house that serves as outside office and lunch space for the employees. Crates of raspberries were piled to the ceiling. The refrigerator shelves had been removed and it was packed with berries. There were 90 crates of raspberries, picked that morning.

Verl explained. A trucker came to pick up a load of nursery stock. He had called ahead and asked if we had a dumpster because his load had shifted and tipped over. He had damaged goods that he needed to throw away. When he arrived and the truck was opened, Verl saw that the damaged goods consisted of raspberries.

They weren't all that damaged. Our crew carefully righted the crates and gently replaced the berries that had not been crushed. These were the ones in the lunch room. The rest had been swept and hosed from the truck. The men all had stained hands and rose-splattered shirts.

But no one was complaining. I drove to the store to get freezer bags. Soon the refrigerator in my kitchen held a huge bowl, all ready for my guests. The freezer was filled with dozens of deep-rose packets. When our employees went home that night, each carried all the fruit he wanted. But there was still a room filled with berries. The remaining ones were more damaged than the ones that had been selected earlier. What to do?

Verl solved the problem. He spent the evening at the lunch room stove, watching the berries while they cooked and sterilizing two five-gallon jugs. He strained the berries into the jugs and inoculated the juice with some of his mother-in-law's best pear wine, a 20-year-old vintage. The next day he carried the jugs into the house and added a syrup of sugar water. I had been instructed to clear a shelf in the utility room and the juice was placed in there. I had no objections. I love wine and my father had always made it. Verl can't drink alcohol. It gives him a headache.

The inoculant was powerful. The juice in the jugs foamed and spilled out of the bottles. I siphoned some off and cleaned up the mess. It took several weeks before all the pans and equipment were returned from the lunch room, and more time before my wine maker friend had scrubbed them and put them away.

The house smells wonderful, if you aren't a temperance worker, as the wine ferments on its shelf by the washer. It tastes good, too. As a child, I used to slip into the barn, lift the cheesecloth from the crocks where Dad's wine was working, brush the fruit flies away and take a large sip from the wooden spoon. Now I siphoned a taste into a wine glass and sipped it lovingly.

My it was good! By Thanksgiving it will be perfect. Come to visit and taste the results of the great raspberry caper.

# *17*

## *Brothers*

Several years after Verl and I were married, my brother came to visit. He had been ill, and while he was recuperating, he decided he could take the time to visit Oregon. I wondered how the visit would go. My brother is very important to me and I hoped that he would also become important to Verl.

"John is an old shoe," I've said, but old sweater is a better metaphor—worn, gray, warm and easy to slip on. His voice, when I call him, comes across the lines like a comforting prayer. "Oh, Sis, that is too bad," when my message is a sad one, and "Gosh, Sis, that is good news. I'm so glad for you," when the word is good.

John is an old soldier. He served in three wars too many. Omaha Beach, Puzon and Saigon are places he has known. When he is asked about his service, he answers briefly and changes the subject.

A veteran of marriages gone wrong, he loved beautiful, unstable women with nurturing passion. Now he is single and no longer smokes or drinks. My daughters say that Uncle John is mellow. I agree. But I know that beneath the relaxed exterior is steel.

He raised his sons and helped raise my daughters. He is Uncle John to the community. He will fix your car, gun or plane, or even make you one. Because he was dyslexic, he has little formal education. But he has hovered around the edges of universities, quietly expressing his talents in basement machine shops. His glory is to fly the planes he has built high above the world, free and competent.

He looked so handsome at my daughter's wedding dressed in a tuxedo and beaming with pride as he escorted her down the aisle. I wish he'd look like that more often. There have been times when I have introduced him to my professional friends that I was sad that he didn't wear his teeth or scrub the grease from under his nails. But let anyone treat my brother with disdain and they were labeled "phony" and crossed off my list of friends.

He arrived at the airport for this important visit and we drove home. I wondered what I would do to entertain him. Verl is always so busy when he is at the nursery.

I needn't have worried. Verl, for the first time, did

only the absolutely necessary things, and he and Johnny played. They went to gun shops and admired guns. John is a gunsmith, among his other talents, and has a fine collection. I hate guns, having been kicked by one as a child, and don't want them in the house. But knowing that men like guns and that perhaps a farmer needs one, I'm tolerant.

They went to farm machinery and nursery equipment businesses. John is a fine mechanic and Verl wanted his advice on equipment. People asked them constantly if they were brothers. I didn't see much similarity except for the gray curly hair and mustaches. But they both do look like my father.

Verl took John to see a friend who had a plane and the two fliers flew together to Mount Saint Helens. John flew the plane into the crater while the owner took pictures. It was a thrill for both of them and they had the added pleasure of being able to show the pictures when this volcano was still news.

Together Verl and John solved the gopher problem. Gophers are a nurseryman's nightmare. Not only do they undermine the fields and create traps for the equipment, but they burrow into the roots of the trees, preventing an adequate rootball when the trees are dug.

Verl had tried conventional means to rid the nursery of these toothy little devils, but they reproduced faster than he could annihilate them. He even got a device that held a shotgun shell. The unsuspecting little animal would come tripping along his subterranean walkway, step on a plate and be blown away. When I learned about this instrument of death, I outlawed it at the nursery. What if a child or a dog stepped on that plate?

The method John and Verl devised was very

effective. They put sulfur in the hole and ignited it with a weed burner. This created sulfur dioxide that was blown through the tunnels by the force of the weed burner and the gophers were gassed in their tunnels. When the men did this, smoke rose from openings all over the fields.

When the visit was over, I drove John to the airport and on the 50-mile ride, we reminisced—about hunting snakes in the swamp, and the Legion/American dances we attended as nervous teenagers, too shy to dance with anyone but a sibling. We talked about all the people we knew from back home.

"Remember old...?" I recalled the joy I had felt when I was called from my bed in the college dormitory to stand in the cold, dark hall and listen to my brother's voice on the telephone. His transport had just landed in New York and he couldn't wait until daylight to call and tell me he was home from World War II. We talked about our parents. John is the only other person alive who knew them well. We didn't say it, but we both were thinking how fast time goes and how lucky we were to have each other.

The day after Johnny left, Verl was on a radio talk show as the expert nurseryman. Listeners called in with questions about a variety of gardening problems and Verl answered them patiently using the botanical and chemical names. He was every bit the educated horticulturist.

Then a listener called to ask, "How can you get rid of gophers?"

Verl's voice raised a bit and he spoke faster. "The best way is to put some sulfur in the tunnel and..."

I chuckled and glowed. The two men I love most had become brothers.

# 18

## Jaime Gets a New Hose

One day we got a call from the clinic where Verl sends the men for medical care. It happened that our mechanic answered the phone. The doctor, desperate to convey the importance of his message, said that Jaime must return for care. "He will die if he doesn't."

Our mechanic rushed out to the field and told Jaime, who was wrestling with a heavy tree, that he was about to die. Jaime rushed back to the doctor mystified, because he felt fine, and terribly frightened.

I called the doctor.

This very concerned physician told me he had arranged for a specialist to see Jaime, but Jaime hadn't kept the appointment. He said that Jaime, who was 21, had a coarctation of the aorta, a congenital stricture that prevented blood from reaching his body unless it was under tremendous pressure. The force in the blood vessels could produce a stroke at any time. Immediate surgery was indicated.

I found Ernesto, who spoke English, and explained Jaime's problem in the most basic terms. Since the men work with irrigation lines and understood water pressure, I used the analogy of a hose to explain the pressure in Jaime's main blood artery. He conveyed the explanation to his cousin.

We had no hospital insurance at that time. Verl had elected to self-insure, to pay the doctor bills. However, this surgery would be beyond our ability. But since it was a life-threatening emergency, perhaps the state would pay. So began a long series of trips to the welfare office.

Jaime spoke no English and he was shy. He was also frightened by the prognosis and puzzled that he could be so sick yet feel so well. I'm not sure he believed what he was being told.

I took Ernesto along to translate the first time we went to the welfare office. I explained the purpose of our visit and was given some forms to fill out. They were in Spanish.

I sat in the crowded welfare office, full of Hispanic and Russian families, flanked by Ernesto and Jaime, and tried to complete the forms. It was soon obvious that the forms were not in Spanish, but in officialese. The jargon was beyond Ernesto's third-grade educational skills. Come to think of it, most officialese is beyond mine. Still I am a health professional and I understood the medical terms, even in Spanish. So I made out the questions as best I could and translated them to English for Ernesto. He translated it into Spanish and Jaime answered. Back it went into English, then I wrote the proper answer on the form in Spanish. All the while our little show was being observed by the others who waited there.

Finally, Jaime, in a leap of faith, signed the forms. Then the three of us trooped into the social worker's office to continue our stand-up comedy routine, a routine which was a matter of life and death.

There were more trips to the office. Ernesto stayed at home and the social worker arranged for a pretty, second-generation secretary to act as a translator. Jaime brightened up when she was around and the communication went easily.

The welfare people were convinced that this was a life-threatening emergency and on that basis they approved the payment of the care. When they told us this Jaime showed no emotion. I thought perhaps he didn't understand. Once we were outside on the sidewalk, we hugged each other with delight and relief.

Next came the trips to the doctors in Portland. Ernesto went once, but he felt he was needed at the nursery. I was forced to use my Spanish to translate for Jaime when a translator was not available.

The hospital was not sure they would accept Jaime as a patient being uncertain about the classification of "life-threatening emergency". Mercifully, Jaime was oblivious to this. I used all my persuasive powers and finally admission for surgery was approved.

I took Jaime to the hospital and sat with him while

he was being admitted and examined. Finally, I said good-bye, kissed him and wished him luck. It was hard to leave that frightened boy there.

The surgery was successful and uneventful except that Jaime was sure that there was a conspiracy to starve him. I told his worried relatives who called from Mexico and Chicago that, *"Jaime esta bien."*

In a month, it was a new Jaime that I took to the doctor. His skin was paler and his lips were rosy instead of purplish. He had studied the English book I gave him and learned enough that he could help me with my faltering Spanish.

Incidentally, we now offer our employees hospital insurance. Though Verl's share of the cost is five times the small fee the employee contributes, several have decided not to be part of the plan. Insurance against a catastrophe they feel will never occur is apparently not important to these young men. It is important to me, however, to know that I will never have to repeat the routine that took place in the welfare office.

# 19

## *Losing Things*

I am convinced that the secret of a happy life is to lose gracefully and move on to other things, persons or ideas to replace the lost ones. Most of us do that because most people are relatively happy.

But how do you deal gracefully with losing your keys, an important form from the IRS or one favorite gold earring? The big things I can handle. It's the little losses that frustrate me.

Verl loses more things than I do and the twitchy,

uncomfortable feeling he experiences as he searches through the garbage can for that important nursery license form communicates itself to me as much as I try to stay aloof from his trivial frustrations.

It's my early conditioning that allows me to get swept up. I'm the child of a mother who never could find her keys and who once lost her bank books for three years. (They were found in the bottom of the garment bag where she had hidden them.)

At least once a week something is lost. It is always important and needed right now. Verl flies through the house like a whirlwind, searching the pile of papers on the section of the kitchen counter assigned to him, scattering the forms that are stacked by his easy chair in front of the television, and creating a storm in his study. By the second time through these places, he begins to wonder if Julie, the long-suffering cleaning lady, has thrown out the lost object.

I inform my spouse that Julie never throws out anything but what is already in the wastebasket. And while he is thinking such crazy thoughts, I want him to know that I never throw out anything, either, so don't think of accusing me. This isn't strictly true, but now is not the time for confession.

Recently, Verl instructed Julie not to empty the wastebasket in his office. She hasn't and we are watching to see how much paper accumulates.

After Verl storms through the house for a while, a strange quiet occurs. That is when I ask, "Did you find it?"

"Yes."

"Where?" I'm ruthless.

"Where I put it."

Now, I must confess that I have lost things. One

morning I did tear through the house looking for the hundred-dollar bill I had stuffed in my sleeve the evening before. Verl had cashed a check for me and gave me the money at dinner. I didn't have a pocket and my purse was in the bedroom, so...

When I couldn't find it anywhere, a fragment of a memory surfaced. The night before I had undressed in the bathroom and just as I flushed the toilet I saw something dark green disappear with the swirling water. Que séra.

Verl called the septic tank man and had the tank flushed. I told him I thought that was foolish and asked how much it cost. He didn't tell me. The money was not found. He did look a little smug. I wonder...

The largest loss was his wallet. Verl likes to carry large sums of money. He says it is convenient. I seldom have more than ten dollars in my purse, using checks or my credit card instead. But my husband will open his wallet and sort through several hundred-dollar bills looking for ten dollars to pay for a movie.

He also carries insurance cards for his vehicles, pesticide, explosive and nursery licenses, and credit cards.

One day a few years ago he plowed one of our fields. He sat all day on the seat of our green John Deere tractor, a helper he affectionately refers to as "my friend Johnny." It is satisfying to turn the rich brown earth over and ready it for planting. At the end of the day he decided to go to the store. He patted his back pant's pocket to check for his wallet.

It wasn't there. It had been there at noon when he had paid for a C.O.D. delivery and he put it back in his pocket. The rest of the day had been spent on the tractor. The conclusion: he had plowed under the

wallet.

He walked the field carefully, inspecting each inch. He told the employees that who ever found it could have the money, $450. Then he replowed the ground, twice! No wallet.

We make jokes now, wondering if it will ever grow. Verl says he knows where it is within two acres. He now uses a wallet with a chain that attaches to his belt. When I lost my dress watch, it was a minor annoyance compared to his loss.

I continue to try to stay out of Verl's way when he has lost something. I don't lecture or laugh, and I try to guard against acquiring his feeling of frustration. When I'm tempted to sort through a pile of papers and discard the useless ones, I don't.

# 20

*Let Me Entertain You*

Giving a party is one of my greatest pleasures. I love parties in general and when I am the hostess I can invite my favorite people. Fortunately, Verl also enjoys being the host.

Shortly after we were married we had our first Hardesty-Holden Hoedown, a large outdoor gathering. That year we invited selected friends. But the next year, when we were besieged by people begging for invitations, we invited everyone—the faculty, the neighbors, relatives, employees and friends. It was potluck, but we supplied the beer, soft drinks, coffee and whatever fruit or vegetable was in season. Our most valuable contribution was Truman Price, a fiddler, and his friends.

We moved all the machinery out of the shed, swept it and placed bails of hay around for seats. Corn meal scattered on the floor made it slippery and our machine shed became a dance hall. Truman brought several musicians with him. One man played a washtub and a rope. When he plucked the rope, the washtub resounded like a bass fiddle. Jane, a friend who has a Ph. D. in chemistry and is thinking of doing a doctorate in the psychology of music, played the violin and sang. Anyone who wanted to sit in with the hired musicians was welcome.

Verl comes from a family of musicians and has inherited all the instruments and talent the family had to offer. An accident twenty years ago severed the ulnar nerve in his left hand, the fingering hand. His skill was diminished by the accident, but he still plays all the old fiddle tunes and at Christmas we hear Fritz Kreisler airs on the viola and carols on the cello. And, of course, at our hoedowns, Verl fiddles.

Since Truman teaches children to square dance, he had no difficulty instructing the folks from the university. Thank heavens he did not demand the perfection the square-dancing clubs insist on. We danced the way I did at the Legion Hall in Mt. Jackson, Pennsylvania when I was a teenager. My friends from Pelham or Boston were delighted to acquire a traditional skill. Our neighbors and employees were happy to exercise their expertise.

When the band struck up a waltz, I would look for

my father-in-law, the best waltzer I have ever known. Mom didn't mind sitting out one dance. I would twirl around with Dad feeling young and beautiful in the arms of this eighty-year-old gentleman. Dad is gone now, but those dances are among my fondest memories of him.

Verl hooked up several of our trucking trailers to a tractor and put bales of hay on the trailer beds as seats for the passengers. Then one of the employees would slowly drive our guests around the nursery. I thought this would amuse the kids, but it was the adults who ran for the seats when the hay wagon appeared.

The kids liked the bark dust and pumice piles. These are the ingredients that are mixed to provide soil for the plants we grow in pots. The children climbed the mountainous piles and slid down with squeals of delight while I worried about splinters and dirt.

There were 250 people at the fifth and last party. We had a small scare and decided to skip a year or two. A newly adopted eight-year-old boy from South America jumped from one of the moving trailers and a wheel ran over his leg. He wasn't hurt and there was no trouble, but it frightened us. Perhaps we could hook up some sort of a seat-belt arrangement and make the hay rides safer. Maybe next year.

We had a Christmas party for fours years inspired by a surplus of a certain variety of tree. Verl had grafted and planted a field of beautiful trees, oriental spruce. This brilliant-green tree has dense, short needles and is very full. When Verl first saw this variety of spruce, he was sure that it was a winner and that customers would love them as much as he. The brokers who visited admired them, but their customers weren't interested. The trees got larger and more

expensive. Verl needed the field to grow more profitable plants. What a shame it would be to grub out and burn those beautiful trees!

A solution presented itself. I invited the Psychiatric Nursing Department and other friends to a party in early December with the additional invitation to cut or dig as many of these trees as they wished. As an added bonus, Verl's sister, Pat, a talented florist, set up a greens shop in the head propagation house, and helped everyone make wreaths and swags.

Pat's birthday is in May close to Mother's Day, and we celebrate these days with a yearly party in the pool room.

Verl built a lap pool for me, an attempt to facilitate exercise. The pool is 64-feet long and the greenhouse that covers it is 100. When the temperature is 60 degrees outside, and it frequently is in early May, the pool room is cozy, a perfect place for a party. The entertainment is provided by Verl's great nieces and nephews who spend the day performing in the pool. Having this party also insures that the pool is clean and ready for my daily swim as soon as the weather permits. I told you that I wasn't above manipulation.

Every other year I spend Christmas with my daughters and their families in Boston or Cincinnati. Since this is a busy time for Verl, he cannot go, and I feel a little sad about leaving him.

But not to worry. I have a family Christmas party before I go. Son Paul was born a week before Christmas and Julie, his wife, arrived shortly after New Year's. Verl's first wife's nieces have similar birthdates and I was born on St. Nicklaus Day, December sixth. We celebrate our births and Christmas and fill the house with good cheer.

When I was working, I would often bring visitors home for dinner. One time it would be a visiting professor from Israel and another my former teachers who were in town for a conference. The invitations would often be spontaneous. I would call Verl and tell him I was on the way. He would rise to the occasion, set the table with the good china, make a centerpiece and begin meal preparation. (Nice man!)

One time I was pleasantly surprised. The meal was ready when we arrived. My guests were from Boston and we all praised Verl for his delicious fried chicken and biscuits. No one was more impressed than I. When dinner was over, Verl drove the guests back to their hotel in Portland and I began the task of cleaning up. I lifted the lid of the garbage can and stared at a pile of Kentucky Fried Chicken containers. Smart man, my husband.

Come to see us. We'll show you a good time, down on the tree farm.

# 21

## Diggers

Some of the nursery-trade publications bear sophisticated titles like *The Pacific Coast Nurseryman* or *Horticulture*. But others have more accurate titles. The publication of the Oregon Association of Nurserymen is *The Digger*. Washington's association calls its magazine *Balls and Burlap*. Many nurserymen (this is a gender-free term since a large number are women) have advanced degrees. Some are executives of large corporations. And yet they are basically farmers, people who put seeds or cuttings in dirt, nurture them and grow a crop.

The field that faces our house is planted with iris bulbs every other year. This is only one of many fields and this business is the largest iris farm in the world, employing hundreds of people. Yet on a recent Sunday, when I looked out and saw a lone tractor making a trail of dust as it traveled back and forth in the field, I recognized the driver, the owner. I wasn't surprised. He either didn't want to ask a worker to work on Sunday or he wanted to be sure it was done right.

Our Mexican employees are puzzled about why Verl works beside them in the fields. They can understand why he takes the truck out to make deliveries since only one other employee, the mechanic, has a license to drive the vehicle. But when they see Verl loading a truck or cultivating a field, they wonder.

Ernesto remarked about it. "Berl, (Spanish speakers have trouble with V) my uncle has six cows and he don't do nothing. Why do you work so hard when you have so much?"

Verl laughed and said, "I work hard. That's why I have this much."

My 59-year-old husband was very tired when he came in one day last spring. He sat at the kitchen table and moaned when he moved.

"What were you doing that made you so tired?" I asked, as a dutiful wife should.

"I was helping the digging crew get that order out. I still dig faster than any of them, but it's getting harder. Those guys are getting fast."

I recalled a time five years before when his father

was still working here. Some weeds close to the trees had grown too large and would have to be hoed. Verl hired a group of local teenage boys to do the hoeing and sent them out with new hoes and his father as supervisor. He told them to see if they could keep up with that 79-year-old man. At the end of the day, I looked out to see Dad walking briskly along trailed by limping boys dragging their hoes.

Operating a nursery is a second career for many people. One of my former students, who has a master's in nursing, became a nurseryman when her children were small because she wanted to work at home. They grew, but by then her new career was more rewarding than the old. I feel a little sad that my profession has lost such a capable person. The nursery association is delighted to have her because she heads the health and safety committees.

The list of former professions reads as though it has been clipped from a dictionary of occupational choices. They include: teacher of classical languages, English professor, history professor, Spanish teacher, mathematician, stock broker and aerospace engineer. Many have degrees in agriculture, but not all are in horticulture. All of them have much in common. If you look at their hands, you will see short, stained nails and calluses. And if you watch them when they talk about plants, their eyes are bright with interest.

There is an acceptance of women in this group more equal than any I have been a part of in the past. Women hold office in the association and are judged on their expertise. There is also a spirit of helpfulness that I find refreshing. Every few weeks there is a call from a fellow nurseryman asking for help. They may ask for advice, to borrow equipment, for a days work from our crew or for help in loading a truck. Help is freely given, and we have the security of knowing that if we need it, it is a phone call away.

These farmers with their grubby nails and interesting pasts are good people.

# 22

*Sharps*

Farms are dangerous places. Public health statistics bear this out. Farm machinery and animals account for the greatest share of injuries and the people hurt most often are the women and children. If you go to a grange meeting or attend a legislative hearing that concerns farmers, you will see men with missing fingers or on crutches. We read with horror newspaper accounts of children who fall from tractors into the paths of a disc and lose arms, or others who lose a hand in corn huskers.

The nursery is not particularly dangerous. We do have our share of strained backs, sore shoulders and pulled muscles, but a few days of light work, some physical therapy and all is well again. Come to think of it, Verl is the one who has had the most injuries of this sort. After two days in the office working to prepare the papers for the new water regulations or working on the taxes, he will rush out and work as hard and fast as our 20-year-old workers. Each time he hurts himself, I am properly sympathetic and he promises to be more careful.

The shovels the men use to dig trees worry me. Verl chooses them with great care. He is interested in the heft and balance, but even more in the steel in the body of the shovel. After he brings them home, he sharpens them by placing them on an anvil and pounding the edges with a ball-peen hammer. They have to be razor sharp to cut through the root of the trees without disturbing the root ball.

I have thought about writing mysteries and one of my favorite scenarios has the murder committed with a sharpened shovel. Another victim in my unwritten drama is done in by eating a tomato from a vine which has been grafted onto a poisonous plant. Let's see, you could dispose of the body in the soil mixer and the remains would fertilize monstrous plants. So much for bizarre thinking.

Fortunately, our workers keep their feet well out of the way of their shovels and they wear heavy work shoes. So we have had no injuries from the shovels.

Grafting season begins shortly after Christmas. The workers sit in the head propagation house at a large table. A wood fire burns in the stove and the room is flooded with fluorescent light. The tape-player blares out music with a Latin beat. Men and women sit in chairs that have been made more comfortable by foam or their favorite pillow from home. All day long they graft trees. Another worker brings the understock to the grafters and carts it away to the greenhouse with the new branches grafted on.

If the grafting is done properly, in a few weeks the new branch will become part of the understock. Several months later, when the plant is healthy and strong, the top of the understock is cut away, leaving the grafted branch that becomes the tree.

In order to do that, sharp knives are needed. Verl buys new grafting knives every year and they are marked with the names of the grafter. The workers become fond of their own tools and don't want to change. Each night after dinner, Verl goes out to the head house to sharpen the knives, a skill that took him years to perfect. With special whet stones, he carefully shapes the edges. Then he tests the sharpness. He plucks one of the fine grey hairs from his head and holds it suspended by one end. If the blade of the knife cuts that hair, he knows he has a good edge.

As you can imagine it is very easy to cut yourself while grafting. The knives are sharper than a surgeon's scalpel and some force is needed to make the cut. Occasionally, we have a year with no accidents. But most years, one or two of our workers will have to be taken to the emergency room for stitches. Fortunately, the cuts are clean and heal quickly. Some of the grafters wear tape on their fingers to protect the most vulnerable spots, but most prefer the freedom of bare hands.

I had never liked sharp knives and my kitchen

knives were always safely dull. This didn't matter when I was peeling vegetables for the two of us. But when we had a larger crowd, I pressed Verl into KP duty. In college, he worked in a cannery and as a house boy. These experiences qualify him as a professional peeler and slicer. My dull knives wouldn't do. And so now my knives are almost as sharp as the grafting knives and I handle them with great care. I have come to appreciate how much faster and easier it is to prepare food if your knife is sharp.

*Pero cuidado!* But be careful!

# 23

## Crash Zone

The settlers, lured by the promise of rich land, reached Oregon before the surveyors. They marked the borders of their homestead claims, planted crops and built fences, houses and barns. When the surveyors arrived and began their work, they found that a map of the homesteaders' claims resembled a crazy quilt rather than a logical grid. Oregon was a long way from Washington, D.C. and the boundaries were left as the farmers had marked them.

Why this bit of history? It explains the unexpected twists and turns of the roads through the flat Willamette Valley. You can drive happily along, enjoying the rippling gold of the ripe wheat, or the clipped green fields of turf farms, and suddenly the road turns right 90 degrees. Then, 100-feet farther on, it turns left.

These S-curves are the sites of many accidents. Our nursery is on one bend of such a curve. Coming from either direction, if you drive straight instead of following the curve, you drive into our driveway. Fortunately, our house if far back from the road and out of reach of drivers frantically trying to control their careening cars.

Our mailbox is not in a safe place, however. Once a month, on an average, it and one of those cars meet head on. Verl grew tired of digging a hole and replacing the post so he found a solution. He welded a steel pipe to a large, heavy metal wheel and placed the mailbox on it. The wheel sits on the ground and its weight firmly anchors the post that holds the mailbox. As a neighborly gesture, he included the box of the little house that shares the curve with us. If a car hits the mailbox, the whole unit tips over. It can be righted easily and if the mailboxes are hammered carefully they can again meet the requirements of the United States Post Office.

There have been bad accidents on the corner and I always rush out to help. You hear the frantic squeal of brakes, followed by a thud and the sound of falling glass. Cars have met head-on on the curve and others have turned over in the ditches and fields. People have been badly hurt. Even though I am a nurse, I have never grown accustomed to the horror of such injuries. I am grateful when I hear the sirens of the ambulances

and know that the paramedics will be assuming responsibility.

One night before Verl and I were married, he was dozing in front of the television. He was awakened by the ominous sounds of a crash on the corner. He pulled on his boots and grabbed the flashlight. Instructing Kristi to call for help he ran through the wet night to the corner.

The road was covered with blood and gore.

Verl was raised on a ranch and spent his childhood castrating cattle and sheep and butchering the rabbits he raised. He is less upset by seeing blood than the average person. But the sight of that road chilled him. Dear God, what had happened to those people!

He swept the fields with the flashlight and it shone on an overturned truck. He ran to it and wrenched open the door. The light flashed on the face of bewildered-looking man. Verl reached in and helped the man out.

"Are you all right?"

"Yeah," the man touched his forehead, "just cut a little. God damn curve. I forgot it was there."

"Are you alone?"

"Yeah."

"Say, what was your load?"

"Oh, I work for the turkey processing plant and take their waste to a mink farm."

Verl began to laugh. "When I saw the stuff on the road...You can imagine what I thought."

Verl then offered the use of the telephone and went in to cancel the ambulance. After that he got out the big fire hose he keeps in the shed and hooked it up to the pump to wash the offal from the road.

One cold winter night just after we had crawled gratefully into bed, we heard the dreaded sounds of a crash. I stuffed my feet into boots and pulled a coat over my robe and hurried down the driveway following Verl's quick steps. It seldom snows in Oregon, but this night there was a wind and a light skiff of snow. A car was positioned directly on top of our overturned mailbox. The wheels were spinning and the motor was roaring but the car was off the ground, held up by our sturdy wheel. Two men were in the car.

I called our, "Are you all right?"

The answer was a torrent of curses.

Verl tried to tell them to stop gunning the motor, that he would get a tractor and pull them off.

The response to his offer was even louder peppered with the F word.

So we two willing Samaritans trudged back to our warm house and called the sheriff to report an accident.

When Verl heard the sirens, he went back to the curve to see if he could help. The police had the situation well in hand. The men, now silent, were handcuffed in the back seat of the police car and a wrecker was towing their car away.

Verl decided that the mailbox repair could wait until the next day and returned to the house and bed.

Once or twice a winter in the Willamette Valley we have black ice. Our normally wet roads look the same whether they glisten with water or ice. When we have black ice, everyone stays at home. However, it can happen quickly and drivers can unexpectedly find themselves driving on a treacherous road. One Thanksgiving eve, just after dark, the temperature dropped suddenly and the wet roads became skating rinks. People were leaving work, some with their cars loaded with groceries for the next day's feast. Kristi was home from college and Paul still lived here. I was preparing dinner. The doorbell rang and a tired-looking man stood there. "I'm in the ditch out by your curve. Could someone help me?"

I called Verl who was in his office in the trailer. As he came down the steps from the little porch, he slipped a bit. Oh, oh, black ice! He got a large chain and hooked it up to one of the big orange tractors. By the time he got out to the road, six cars had joined the first one. As they had rounded the banked curve, they had slid helplessly down the slope into the ditch. Paul had joined Verl at that point.

Verl hooked up the chain on the car bumper and pulled the first car back to the road. Then Paul helped the driver put on his tire chains. By the time he drove cautiously down the road, more cars had been added to the crowd in the ditch.

Verl and Paul were at the road helping motorists for several hours. They refused the money that was offered and sent a score of grateful people on their way. When they came back in the house, Verl's nose was red and it was dripping into his mustache. Paul's hands were bruised and numb with cold. But the fellows were high with the pleasure of helping.

As we sat down to dinner, I thought of a line from a poem my father used to recite: "Let me live in my house by the side of the road/And be a friend to man." We toasted each other with Grandma Knox's pear wine, filled our plates with our reheated dinner—and silently thanked God for our blessings.

# 24

*Far Away*

The day before yesterday hurricane Bob blew across new England. All afternoon, as I listened to the news reports, I felt as if a cold hand were clutching my heart. My daughter, Shevawn, my son-in-law and their three little boys live on the south shore of Boston Harbor in the path of the storm. I kept thinking of the sycamore tree, hundreds of years old, that spreads its long branches over their roof. When I called the phone rang but then no one answered, not even the answering machine.

The next day Shevawn called. All was well. Their electricity had been restored and the phone was now working. The storm had pruned the tree of its weaker limbs without damaging the roof. Elizabeth, the woman who cares for Shevawn's children while she works, had called her son. He was busy sawing up the branches and raking the yard.

After I talked with Shevawn, I spoke with Elizabeth. There is a bond between us. She is doing what I might have done in an earlier time, helping to raise my grandchildren. A wise woman, a veteran of 12 births, Elizabeth tells me the day-by-day details of my grandsons' lives and helps me to feel included. I am grateful.

It's hard to be so far away from the boys and my granddaughter in Cincinnati. I visit often, talk on the phone and write letters. Leslie and Louis are old enough to send me letters and kindergarten artwork. My refrigerator is decorated with my trophies of grandmotherhood. But I wish I lived closer.

I miss sharing the day-by-day lives of my daughters and their children. When my girls were growing up, my mother was nearby and the four of us were a tight little group. When my brother, John, came home from Vietnam, he became part of the circle. Even though my daughters' father was not present and not important to their daily lives, we had a close-knit family.

My values, passed down from my Scots-Irish ancestors, include a strong belief in the necessity for the individual to set the direction of his own life. Children are trained to be independent. Parents are not to become burdens to their children. Paradoxically, along with these values exists a deep loyalty to family.

I was the one who moved to enhance my career. I told myself that the girls were free to do the same. When they finished college, they might have gone to California or to a job overseas. They met their husbands in college and settled in the states where they went to school.

I have become aware of new feelings along with the twinges of guilt and the pangs of longing. My interest and affection for young women who are dealing with the same problems my daughters face are heightened. And I am positively a fool over babies.

The young women to whom I am closest spatially are the three women who work at the nursery. They have become important to me. They are special people in their own right, and I am sure I would be fond of them even if my daughters lived nearby. But my appreciation of their lives is keener in these circumstances.

Carmen, Isidra's daughter, is eight. She is a beautiful child with clear skin, long, dark hair and bright eyes. He manners are those of the most gracious adult.

She often comes to work with her mother and in the summer we swim together in my pool twice a week. She comes into the house and reads or watches television if she wishes. I speak English with her because she needs to increase her vocabulary. Most of the time when we are together, I am in the grandmother mode. But occasionally we become two eight-year-old girls and play together. She addresses me as Mrs. Florence. When she writes me notes, I am *Dona* Florence.

Does my affection for the people who are spatially close to me lessen my love for my own family? No, it enhances it. Listening to Carmen helps me to understand what all little girls, including Leslie, are thinking about. It also makes me appreciate the intellectually rich environment my daughter and son-in-law provide for my granddaughter. I try to bring some of the same richness to Carmen.

Since I never had sons, and Paul was a very mature teenager when I married Verl, I haven't had experience raising boys. When the workers drop by with their little sons, I watch the boys climb the bark-dust pile, skin their knees and conquer their tears, and think, "Just like the grandsons."

It is not necessary to have children or grandchildren of one's own to appreciate all children. Some of my friends who have devoted their lives to the care of sick children are childless. But for me, loving my daughters and their children deeply and missing them helps me realize how precious all daughters, sons and children are.

# 25

## A Nurseryman in Paris

A year after we were married, Verl and I went to Europe. It was the first time he had been in that part of the world. He had spent two years in Japan and Korea when he was in the Air Force but there had been no other trips abroad. A portion of this trip was spent with a group from the medical school, but we were on our own for most of the trip, clutching our Eurorail passes, ready for adventure.

I saw the countries I had seen before with new eyes

when I was with Verl. We were on a tour bus in Geneva when he called, "Stop! Stop!" to the driver. As the driver pulled to the curb, Verl jumped up from his seat and rushed to the front of the bus to photograph the largest and oldest *cedrus atlanticu* he had ever seen. "It must have been more than 300 years old, "he explained to the startled doctors.

I hung onto his coattails when we were on a train going up to the top of the Jungfrau. I detected the same wild-eyed excitement as he looked through the windows. "Look, look at the mugo pine!"

I looked. It looked just like the mugo pine he grafted and put in our greenhouses. But of course these small shrubs were native to the high Alps and had propagated naturally.

He went wild in Versailles, about both the statuary and the plants. He was intrigued by the yews, centuries old, that had been snipped into small cone-shaped bushes. Watching and learning from Verl, my own world expanded.

We arrived in Paris in the afternoon on a train from Switzerland. In the station, we consulted our travel book and picked a hotel not far from the Champs 'Elysées and the Arc de Triomphe. Then we found a cab, went to the hotel and got a room. By the time we checked in and dropped our bags, we were congratulating ourselves. We really were world travelers.

First stop was the Arc de Triomphe. We stood on the top and admired the city. But I must confess, Verl was more impressed with the skill of the French drivers who raced round the edifice. The arch sits in the middle of a traffic circle and six boulevards lead into the circle. From the safety of our perch, we watched the traffic mayhem below us.

Finally, we descended and sought rest in a sidewalk café. We sat at a table at the edge of the sidewalk. It was the drugstore cowboy area and Verl was wearing a western style suede jacket, blue jeans and cowboy boots. He was comfortable in the clothes he wore at home but he was unmistakenly American. There were about 35 others sitting at the tables outside.

We ordered drinks and relaxed, tired but pleased with ourselves. Suddenly, my husband leaped to his feet and shouted into the face of an old man with a cane who was passing by the table. "Damn you, watch your dog."

Conversation at the other tables ceased. Thoughts raced through my head: my God, an incident in a foreign country! The small dog the man had on a leash sat patiently by his master's feet. The Frenchman was screaming back at Verl. I don't speak French, but it sounded like swearing to me.

"What happened?"

"His damn dog pissed in my boot."

Between giggles I said, "You have another pair of jeans. We can wash those. And your boots have been wet before."

Then Verl began to laugh. Relief washed over me as laughter swelled from the other tables. The old man continued to sputter and swear.

Verl sat down and the old gentleman shook his cane at the audience and shuffled off with his dog.

No international incident. Just a good story to take home.

# 26

## A Few Bad Apples

At this moment, Verl has one reliable employee who is an unhyphenated American. In the past, there have been other good workers who stayed with us for a short time and then moved on to higher-paying, less physically demanding jobs. A group of local house-wives handled the propagation for five years. They stayed because Verl allowed flexible hours and because the only marketable skills they had at that time were ones Verl had taught them.

Most of our Anglo employees have been men on probation, alcoholics whose job history was so bad they could not get other work, or people who had chronic problems.

There was Jim, a 40-year-old carpenter with several drunk-driving convictions. He begged for a job. He'd do anything, he said. Verl hired him. He was good with machinery and he did some repairs around the place. Since his license to drive had been suspended, his wife, Lou, had to drive him to work. She asked for a job and joined the other women in the propagation house.

One Monday I went out where the women were working and there was Lou, her eye blackened and her jaw swollen. She had fallen down the stairs, she said. Two weeks later, she injured her thumb—at work, she said. Strange, she hadn't said anything to the other women when it happened. Any injury a worker receives on the job is tallied by the worker's compensation carrier eventually increasing the cost of compensation insurance.

I voiced my concerns over lunch. "Verl, I'm sure Jim is drinking and beating Lou."

"Yeah, maybe. But how am I going to prove Lou didn't hurt her thumb here. Besides, I need him to enclose the machine shed."

I let the matter drop.

One Friday night we came home from the movies and found Jim's car at our gas pump. There was Jim pumping stolen gasoline into his car.

"My mother just died and I have to get to the funeral. I didn't have money for gas because Lou paid the rent tonight and went to get groceries. I didn't think you'd mind if I borrowed some gas."

Verl didn't mind under the circumstances. In fact, he even gave Jim an advance on his salary to make the trip. Gosh, the paycheck had disappeared quickly. He had just been paid that afternoon.

Jim and Lou were gone for a week. When they returned, Jim asked if he could see me just once as a patient because there was something he was very upset about. Seeing an employee was not a good idea, but since he said it was a crisis and it would only be once, I said all right.

He came into my office, sat on the couch and began a long, rambling story about having had a precognition of his mother's death and having had dreams about seeing her in her coffin before she had actually died. People often have precognitions, but few see a therapist about it. I didn't know what he wanted from me. I told him that such experiences were unexplainable but happened to normal people. I offered support and tried to get him to talk about how he felt about his mother and what losing her meant. Nothing seemed to reach him. He didn't smell of alcohol, but he did seem intoxicated. I have been a psychiatric nurse for 30 years and and psychotherapist for 25. I never saw such a confusing patient. I though I was being had, that Jim was manipulating me to gain sympathy from his boss's wife. But I wasn't sure, so I didn't confront him.

Several months later, when Verl entered the propagation house, one of our employees, a Cuban woman who was a Jehovah's Witness, announced dramatically that a miracle had occurred.

"Why, what happened?" he asked not sure this wasn't a prelude to a sermon.

"Yeah," said another propagator, a local housewife. "Jim's mother just walked in looking for him."

Verl didn't have to make a decision about firing Jim. That weekend he was picked up for drunk-driving, the last of a string of convictions that sent him to prison. We saw him later at the State Fair. He had been paroled. He was on antibuse as a condition of his parole and was working in Portland. Verl and he had a nice conversation while I stood there gritting my teeth. I am sure other people who have sat in my office have not always told me the truth, but Jim had deliberately lied to me and I knew it.

Another employee who left a lasting impression was Joe. Joe was a middle-aged hippie. He arrived seeking work at a busy time and was hired. He asked if he could pitch a tent down in the woods by our pond for a few days. His wife had insisted he leave and he lacked money for rent. He made camp and stayed for months, until we fired him. He entertained friends there, and his teenage son arrived from California to spend his school vacation with Daddy at his camp by the pond.

Our house needed painting. Joe said he could paint, so Verl hired him to do that task. First the house was to be washed with a high-pressure hose. I heard the sound of the hose one summer morning as I drank my tea and read the paper. Then I heard the disturbing drip of water.

I rushed into the living room to find streams of water coming in around the door and windows, spraying the walls and the oil painting of my grandfather, soaking the oriental rugs and forming puddles on the parquet floor. My first impulse was to open the door, but I thought better of that and resorted to pounding and screaming. Finally, Joe moved his hose away from the door and I wrenched it open to deliver a blast of anger.

I rushed to my study to find my computer awash and a copy of a novel I was ready to send out soaked. The water had come through the louvered window. The water was coursing down beams and dripping all over the house.

I admit that I swore at Joe, the first time I've ever done that to an employee—or anyone other than a husband or child, people with whom one has swearing privileges. He just looked at me with a vague quizzical look. Joe later reported to Verl that I was a "little upset."

Then I watched him paint the house. He started with the black trim. Then he painted the gray siding. Of course, he had to go back and touch up the black where the gray had splattered. Finally, he painted the underside of the broad eaves, white of course, spattering white on both the gray and black. Then another touchup.

I tried not to look, but it seemed that every time I glanced out the window I saw Joe, with a dreamy look on his face, patiently touching up what he had painted a few days before. When I talked with him, he told me he had done oils and studied art at one point. Verl would admit that drugs had fried his brain—just a little. I wasn't sure he had ever had one.

Verl thought there was hope for Joe. When he finished the house, he went back on the nursery's payroll. We went on vacation and Verl instructed Joe to do the watering, a vital function when plants in the can yard, thousands of dollars worth, could die if they weren't watered for two days.

We were in Boston when we got a call that our burglar alarm had been set off. Joe had tried a door to make sure it was locked. A series of calls followed, to the police, to family to get it reset, etc. Then we got a call from Ernesto. He had come over Sunday morning to use the phone and found that the watering was not being done, and that Verl's new truck, which the employees were not to drive, was missing. So was Joe.

Another call. Joe had returned. He had taken the truck and his son to eastern Oregon and it broke down. He left it there and hitchhiked home. Verl flew home immediately, buying a new airline ticket, losing the price of the return ticket and fired Joe.

Eric was around for along time in spite of my warnings that he wasn't to be trusted. A handsome blond man in his early twenties, he confided to Verl that he was on probation from Texas for child abuse. The child had been taken away from him and Tammy, his common-law wife. He was very contrite about this.

I did marital counseling as well as psychotherapy in my practice and Eric asked if he could make an appointment for himself and Tammy. The antenna that I have in my brain picked up manipulation vibes and the experience with Jim was still fresh. I told him no because it would be difficult to maintain objectivity when he worked for my husband. He begged, but I held firm and referred him to a colleague of mine. He did not make an appointment.

Tammy became pregnant and a beautiful little boy was born. In a year, she had Eric arrested for child abuse and the baby was taken from them. In another year, a daughter was born and although the Children's Services Division has investigated, she is still with them.

Eric was always smiling, calling across the yard to me in a manner so friendly I felt uncomfortable. But

Verl liked Eric. He was good with machinery, he could do plumbing and he understood our complicated irrigation system. And he flattered Verl and entertained him.

Verl lent money to him to buy a house trailer and gave him advances on his salary whenever he asked. Eric was fired a few times because he didn't show up for work regularly. But a few days later there he would be, calling, "Hello there, Florence. Don't you look nice today!"

I extracted a promise from Verl that Eric would no longer be in the nursery, but Eric stayed and I stopped complaining. (I have found that there is a direct relationship between the amount of nagging I doand the amount of time it takes to get my desires fulfilled.)

A year passed and we went on vacation. All apparently was well and we thought that perhaps, finally, we could leave without fearing that the sky would fall. When we returned, Verl made the rounds to inspect the nursery. He found that ten cords of seasoned oak firewood were gone from the shed on my farm. He asked the man who rented the house if he had seen anyone take it.

The tenant said, "Yes, Eric came every evening last week and hauled a load away. He was driving your green truck."

Verl called the sheriff and that was the end of Eric's employment at the nursery. When his sentencing was in the paper, people came to Verl and told him that they had bought nursery stock from Eric thinking it was from Verl. We found that he had sold quite a few of our tools as well.

Eric is on probation and is supposed to make restitution. He did give Verl $50. Then Tammy called me and asked that we return the money so that they could have a nice Christmas. Mrs. Scrooge hung up on her.

When I read in the paper that Mexican immigrants are taking jobs away from American workers, I think of Eric, Jim and Joe, and say, "Thank heavens for the Mexicans."

# 27

## The Girls

We were driving down the road on a sunny spring day. We passed a grass field where several hundred sheep grazed, mothers and their spring lambs. Verl slowed and we admired the woolly creatures.

I've been thinking." Verl said, "if we put sheep down by the pond, maybe they would clear out the brush."

"Yes, it looks like a park over on Steven's place where he keeps his sheep." I was excited by the prospect.

The idea remained and we began to add more knowledge to it. A family who I saw for marital counseling raised sheep as well as turkeys. I learned a lot more about turkeys than I wanted to know, but when sheep were mentioned, I was very interested. I made an effort to ask sheep questions on my own time so my clients didn't pay for my interest. I bought books and Verl and I studied them. One of my students raised sheep and spun the wool. I arranged to have lunch with her when the opportunity arose.

My grandfather had been a sheep man in Pennsylvania and my mother had entertained my brother and me with stories about her pet ewe named Money. Incidentally, I never tasted lamb until I was an adult. Mother never served it.

One evening as my turkey-sheep-grower client left my office, he stopped to talk with my husband who was mowing the lawn. When Verl came in, he said that he had bought 14 sheep for $25 apiece.

In classical psychoanalytic circles such a transaction is forbidden. But when one practices in a rural area, one does not have the luxury of maintaining the prescribed distance between client and therapist. Client-therapist is often not the only relationship I have with my clients. The client might also be my doctor, my minister or my friend.

Verl brought the sheep home in a truck and they tripped down the ramp on high-heeled hooves and into our hearts. The 14 one-year-old ewes, Suffolk-Hampshire crosses had fussy bodies and black faces and feet. They were skittish and followed whichever one of the group made the first move. Yet they were tame and curious. They reminded both Verl and me of a

crowd of female high-school students. An hour after they arrived, they became "the girls."

They liked their new home down by the pond, but they didn't do much to clear the brush. In fact, Verl had to rescue one of the girls who got tangled in blackberry brambles and couldn't escape.

Another time he heard mournful bleating and investigated. Thirteen of the ladies were crying out in sympathy for the fourteenth who had made her way to a ledge on the brink of the pond and couldn't get back up the bank. Verl climbed down and began hoisting this hundred-pound, frightened female up the steep bank. He was pushing from behind, about the level of his head while the poor sheep searched for footing. The back hoof connected and she shoved off, leaving a print and bruise on her rescuer's face.

Sheep need shots against worms, foot rot and various other maladies. Verl bought the medication and two syringes and fourteen needles. I was a little worried about the sterility of the technique, but agreed to administer the injection. Verl wrestled the first woolly lady to the ground and I inserted the needle in the soft skin under her foreleg. The others followed of their own accord. After all, they did everything as a group.

Verl and I would walk down to the pond in the evening carrying a white bucket with a sheep treat, special vitamin-filled grain. My husband would start to baa and the girls would answer him and start heading toward the gate. By the time we arrived, they would be jostling each other for the best position to receive the goodies.

One time I went down alone and went inside the pasture. I wanted to pet them when I gave them their treat. As soon as they saw the white bucket, they ran toward me and began to crowd close. One pushed against my knees from the behind and another pushed from the front. Bucket, sheep and I ended in a tangle on the ground. I threw the bucket away from the crowd and they followed it while I got up, brushed myself off and escaped outside the fence.

The white-bucket technique served Verl well the time they escaped from their pasture. Their yen to eat the alfalfa in the neighbor's field was just too much for the fence. The neighbors called us and Verl arrived to see three men trying to herd our skittish girls back through the hole in the fence. One fellow was on a three-wheeler trying to play cowboy (sheep boy) to no avail. Verl called baa, held the bucket high, and 56 black hooves turned his way and dashed through the fence for the treat.

I was content to allow the girls to remain in permanent adolescence, but my farmer husband felt that propagation was indicated. A neighbor had a prize Shropshire ram that had feet too sore for him to be shown at the fair. He brought the fine fellow over and we put him in the pasture with the girls.

They seemed to be totally uninterested in him and he tagged along behind them like a little brother they were forced to watch. He stood apart when they got their treats, standing like a dandy on his dainty hooves. I imagined that he had a pained look on his face, as though his feet hurt. (Foot rot is painful, so I was probably right.)

But he did his duty, and in February our girls brought forth 26 lambs! I had studied the book on difficult lamb deliveries and was prepared for obstetrical experience. But the girls came through and did it all themselves. I did find one little body, the wool stiff with amniotic fluid, wedged underneath a sliding door. It must have been delivered when the mother was lying against the door. Since all the ewes had twins, we never knew which one had lost a lamb.

The behavior of the girls changed the instant they gave birth. They left the skittish adolescent group and joined the young matron crown. The mothers stayed apart from the singles and lounged together, nursing or watching their young play at being big sheep. Their behavior was like my own when I would sit in a neighbor's yard, drink coffee and watch our toddlers play together in the sandbox.

We did have our tragedies, however. One night before the sheep lambed, our tenants called us to say that dogs were chasing the sheep. Verl went to the other farm and found that one sheep had been mauled to death. Another had been torn by the dogs, but was so terrified that he couldn't get near it. The dogs had disappeared. He shut the sheep in the barn and came home to tell me the sad news.

The next morning we went to the barn. The injured ewe had had the front of her chest torn, so the the skin hung almost to the ground, revealing all the muscles and the joints of her forelegs. I was sick when I saw her. But she was walking around and eating in spite of her horrible injuries. Verl said "no" when I suggested a vet. He was not willing to spend hundreds of dollars to save a $25 animal. It had to be do-it-yourself surgery.

I came back to the house and boiled up a curved rug needle, scissors and tweezers. I could find nothing to serve as a needle-holder and finally threw a pair of pliers in the boiling water. I found some strong silk buttonhole thread and tossed it in also. Armed with the instruments, clean towels, cotton balls and determination, I returned to the pasture. After all, I had assisted with suturing scores of times. I told myself, I can handle it.

Verl caught the sheep and Paul talked to our girl with a soothing voice. I inserted the needle in the holder, and said a prayer and began. The sheep never moved.

It was rough going. Sheep skin is tougher than human skin and there was the wool to contend with. My hands are small and not particularly strong, "Here, let me do it," Verl said. "My hands are stronger than yours. Tell me what to do." So my assistant took over the surgery and with his large, calloused hands gently stitched up the wound. I gave our girl a penicillin injection and when she was released, she got up and ran to join her friends.

About three days later maggots appeared in the wound. I called my client for advise and he said that the maggots must go or she would surely die. Some insect spray took care of the infestation.

The wool on the sheep's chest came off and was replaced by black short hair. A short time later, she gave birth to twins and nursed them without difficulty. Because of the distinctive marking, we could identify her. It soon was apparent that she was the head sheep, the one that led the flock through the fence into the neighbor's fields and was first in line for treats. She had become our favorite.

The dogs attacked again at noon. The sheep were saved by a lucky circumstance. A private detective was driving down the road and saw two large dogs, one a chow, chasing the terrified animals. The sheep ran for the barn, their place of security, but the dogs followed them in. The detective parked, crossed the fence and arrived just in time to prevent slaughter. He took photographs of the dogs and followed them to their homes where he photographed them again.

The county dog control officer picked up the dogs and they were sentenced to death. The owner of the chow was a friend of Verl's and he appealed the verdict. He came to us begging for his pet's life. Two animals with the same description had been killing calves and sheep in the area for several years. This time the photographs were proof that these two were killers. We had chows when I was a child and they are my favorite dog. But the image of the placid ewe with her chest torn open hardened my heart and the dogs were destroyed.

We kept the sheep for three more years, adding Rommy, a beautiful Romney ram, to the flock. His wool was almost as soft as cashmere and five inches long. But after that incident with the dogs, we were never without fear that we would come home from a trip or wake up some morning to a massacre. We were planning a vacation in England and concern about the sheep was intense. The man who sheared them for us knew what a productive flock they were. When he offered us a good price for them, we consented. I felt as if I were saying good-bye to old friends when they were loaded on the truck.

I stop my car along the country road in the spring and sit and watch the lambs and their mothers. But I control my nostalgia and drive on. I have tried to eat lamb, but even ground up in a favorite Greek dish, it is impossible to swallow it. Next to cats, sheep are my favorite animals. But I am glad that cats are now my only pets.

# 28

## *Silty Soil Or Darn Dirt*

It covers the furniture like a soft veil; hunks of it rest on the hall carpet. If you run your finger over my books or window sills, you will note that your digit is soft gray. A fine powder rests on the kitchen chair where Verl sits and is camouflaged by the cream color of his leather chair. It coats the cars, clogs the down spouts and blows in the wind. I call it dirt.

But to my farmer spouse, this substance is silty clay loam—good soil. It isn't number one soil, that rare prize all farmers lust for, but it is good number two soil, full of nutrients, well drained and easy to work. It contains enough clay to hold the root balls of the trees he digs together and to protect the roots from transplant shock. It is deep enough so that we never have to worry about the topsoil being depleted.

There are no stones on our farm, except the gravel that is trucked in for the road and for the beds the potted plants rest on. When we traveled to New England and saw the rocks the farmers there have to contend with, we wondered why the Pilgrims ever stopped there. In Ireland, we looked at the rock-strewn fields and thanked our ancestors for leaving that rugged terrain. When Verl does find a stone, there is a good possibility that it is a tool left by the Indians who, hundreds of years ago, camped along the creek that runs through the farm. We have a collection of pounding and cutting stones that were the tools of the first inhabitants of this land.

When I first met Verl, he administered a test to decide if I would be a suitable wife. We were standing in the courtyard of my new condominium discussing landscaping possibilities. I was taking Verl to the opera with my season tickets and we were dressed in our best. I was in blue silk and he looked very handsome in a dark blue suit that showed off his silver curls. He reached down and picked up a handful of soil, rubbed it with both hands and sniffed it. He said, "It has a lot of clay, but we can lighten it up by adding perlite." Then he reached out his hand to give me this substance.

I recoiled and said, "I don't want to get my hands dirty."

He dropped the soil, brushed his hands together and put them in his pockets.

I protested, "Don't, you'll get your pockets dirty."

He went into the house and washed his hands. I didn't know that I had failed a test. But he married me in spite of my aversion to dirty hands. As a nurse, I have spent years washing my hand so that they would be germ-free for each new patient. I like clean hands.

Dirt shows up in strange places in our house. Sometimes the doorknobs are crusted with dried soil. If Verl uses my car, which happens as little as I can manage it, the steering wheel might feel gritty under my squeamish fingers. When I ride in one of the trucks, I know I will be sitting on a cover impregnated with soft, powdery soil.

And then there are the clothes. During digging season, especially if it is wet, Verl's jeans are encrusted with grayish dirt. I take them out to the patio and sweep them before I put them in the washing machine. I'm sure our septic tank contains a ton of well-washed dirt.

At night, when my handsome husband undresses, sometimes I chuckle. His white underwear will bear evidence that sometime that day he had rushed into the bathroom wearing his rain gear—yellow waterproof pants and shirt—over his jeans and jacket, and in his hast to relieve himself had no time to wash his hands. The black stains around the strategic area of his shorts are impossible to remove completely, although bleach does turn them faint gray.

I tease about the dirt and occasionally scold, but I am a farmer's wife and I do appreciate the life-giving properties of the soil. When I look at a field of our beautiful blue spruce trees, so full and straight, I know that they have three times as much growth each year as trees grown elsewhere. Part of this can be attributed to the mild climate, the rain and my husband's skill. But much of the growth is because that substance that I sometimes call dirt gives them what they need to be healthy.

# 29

## An Interesting Party

One of my former students, a Silverton woman, invited Verl and me to her graduation party. Sandy was in her thirties, married and with children when she decided to become a nurse. She had to work part time and commute to Portland, to complete her education. When I would meet her in the halls of the university, she would tell me about her latest triumph or trial and I became very fond of her. Finally, she was to graduate and she wanted me to be part of the celebration.

The party was an outdoor affair and the invitation had been issued by a woman named Liz. When Verl and I arrived at the party, we were greeted on the front porch of the farmhouse by the hostess. I discovered then that Liz was someone I knew very well. She and her husband, a prominent attorney, had used my services as a marriage counselor. After a few sessions they had stopped coming. And now Liz was divorced and using her maiden name.

Patients or clients frequently do not acknowledge knowing their therapist if they meet them in another setting. While lawyers, bankers and other professionals are careful not to reveal their clients' secrets, they are not faced with the problem of how to greet someone you know very well as though he were a stranger.

Liz solved my problem by greeting me warmly. She introduced herself to Verl and we continued through the farmhouse to the large back yard where the party was in progress.

It was a warm summer evening, a rare event in Oregon, where the temperature can drop 40 degrees from noon to midnight. Twenty or so people were scattered around the lawn chatting or attending to the barbecue.

Sandy, the honored guest, rushed forward to greet me, and we introduced our husbands. Then the other guests came forward with exclamations of delight.

"Florence, it is wonderful to see you," "Florence, we want you to meet our children." I was kissed and hugged and swept to a place of honor and seated. Verl followed behind looking a though he had forgotten something.

When I was seated, someone rushed off to get me a beer. One young man, Tony, began, "Well, I am still flying for United, but I've learned how to handle it. You'd be proud of me."

The reports continued.

"I'm in school now and doing well..."

"My mother-in-law is coming next week and I am actually looking forward to it..."

"We are going to have a baby in the spring..."

Seven of the ten couples who were there had been my clients. They weren't all glad to see me. Two husbands got very busy with the barbecue and greeted me as a stranger.

While these clients talked with me as though I were an old friend, I still had to be careful. It was possible that they did not know that the other couples had consulted me, and very likely did not want the others to know that they had.

I also was aware that the group was interested in Verl. I had been a role model for many of the women and now they were meeting the man I had married.

Did I detect a mischievous gleam in my husband's eye? He wouldn't!

Please, Verl, I thought, don't tell them your Mr. Bang stories. And don't tell them about the time I flushed $100 down the toilet.

Verl, a socially aware gentleman, behaved as one should when one is confused in a social setting. He smiled a lot and kept his mouth shut.

I do have clients who have become friends. In fact, I get letters from people who consulted me when I lived in New York state almost twenty years ago. But I never had met so many at one time in one place, unexpectedly.

A pleasant, if somewhat wary, evening passed. I introduced myself to the reluctant husbands at the barbecue and put them at their ease. I was happy to hear that most of these very nice people were doing well with their lives. Then, as soon as it was socially correct, I signalled Verl and we began moving among the guests to say good-bye.

In the car I said, "Don't ever tell anyone, but most of those people were my former clients."

"I guessed that. At first I wondered how you knew everyone so well and I'd never heard of them. Don't worry, I'll never tell."

"And thanks, Honey, for not telling any of your jokes or stories about me."

"Not in that hotbed of Florence fans! I'll save my stories for the nursery crowd."

# 30

## To See Or Not To See

Those of us who were fortunate enough to have escaped nearsightedness in our childhood, are faced with increasingly dim near vision in our middle years. It goes with graying temples and laugh lines. We all know that, but the degree of acceptance varies.

I was a young 44 when I finished my doctorate, young enough that I had to discourage several book salesmen in their late twenties who visited the school where I taught. A colleague came to see me and I proudly handed her a bound copy of my dissertation. She whipped out a pair of granny glasses and perched them on her nose before she opened the volume.

"Helen, what happened? When did you start needing those?"

"About a month ago. They are wonderful. Here try them."

I gingerly accepted them and slid them on. I picked up a book and looked. "Good heavens! It is all so clear. I must need them too."

An optometrist confirmed this. I didn't want half glasses, though. They reminded me of Grandma and Santa Claus. I got a pair of gold-rimmed bifocals, the top part of which was clear. I could look at my lecture notes and then look at my students without the distraction of putting on or removing glasses.

I didn't need to wear them full time until two years ago. The transition was not painful. If wearing glasses was the price I had to pay for seeing the world clearly, it was a small one.

My husband is younger than I, but that only partially explains the resistance he has had to wearing glasses. He started out not being able to read the menu when we were in restaurants. At first, I handed him my glasses so he could make an informed choice. But after a while, I began to resent passing over to him what had become so much a part of my persona.

So he went to a local discount store and bought himself a supply of granny glasses. They were strewn around the house and his office and were never where he needed them. But he did recognize that the little plastic devices enabled him to see more clearly.

I persuaded him to go to our health maintenance organization, have an eye examination and get some bifocals. He did. He even got trifocals—and lost them somewhere in the fields two days later. Probably not far from the spot where he plowed under his wallet.

He hasn't been back to the health maintenance organization for glasses or an examination since. Somewhere down deep he seems to feel that it was all their fault. He has visited an optometrist and does have a prescription that enables him to buy granny glasses at the discount store with more knowledge.

The frames of his glasses break often and he mends them with masking tape, safety pins or a great big glob of yellow glue from the hot-glue gun. He saves an intact pair for special occasions when he wants to make an impression. Most often, however, he forgets to take them with him and is forced to borrow a friend's—or mine. I tried to avoid nagging and kept telling myself that he has a right to make his own decisions about this.

I bought a new computer several years ago and found that I had to bend my head backwards and sit on the edge of the chair to bring the screen into proper focus. I made a trip to the optometrist and got trifocals. That problem was solved.

But my new glasses forced me to face a shocking realization. Before trifocals, I made up my face in the bathroom without my glasses, staring into the mirror across the counter. I saw a pleasant round face in the mirror and when I applied a touch of color to the cheeks and eyes, I looked as I had looked for years. When I put on my bifocals, the face that I saw from a distance of four feet was the same.

The first day after I got my new trifocals, I stared in the mirror at a face that had aged ten years. With the middle range of my vision clear, the veil was lifted and wrinkles and chins appeared. Now I don't put on my glasses until I have turned away from the mirror.

Come to think of it, Verl must see me as I saw myself before trifocals. Maybe his vanity or resistance to being dependent on little plastic lenses is not irrational after all. I haven't nagged him about his glasses for a while and I even carry an extra pair of granny glasses in my purse, in case he needs them.

# 31

*Amsterdam*

Verl and I traveled to Holland several summers ago.
We were part of a small group of nursery people who
were invited by a nursery equipment manufacturer to
observe the mechanization of the industry that has
occurred in the Netherlands. We stayed at an inn in a
small town, and every day for five days we were on the
bus at seven and off to tour nurseries. Every night at
seven we dragged ourselves off the bus, through an
empty bar full of moth-eaten stuffed animals, to our

rooms and sleep.

We were overwhelmed with what we saw: acres and acres of glass greenhouses costing millions of dollars; machines with metal fingers that lifted delicate cuttings out of trays and replanted them in others, watering and fertilizing them in the process; machines that took scores of potted plants into the greenhouse and set them in neat rows, properly spaced; greenhouses where millions of perfect red peppers were produced without soil.; huge nursery operations staffed by two or three people. Over dinner and in our dreams we calculated the cost of the machines against the savings they would offer.

When the stimulating and exhausting week was over, we had a free day in Amsterdam. The group scattered, but Verl and I found ourselves with two of our favorite people, a young couple, both nurserymen.

Matt and Happy are in their thirties. Matt is a tall, smiling Oklahoman and Happy is a petite Chinese woman. They met at graduate school where they were studying plant pathology and married to begin a family and a business.

Matt truly never meets a stranger. His warm, blue eyes, his apple cheeks and smile draw everyone to him. On the tour, he greeted everybody he met with the same open warmth. Conversations always developed and Matt asked questions that most of us would hesitate to ask a stranger. But the responses were as open and freely given as the questions. Happy, a name that sounds somewhat like her Chinese name, is also a charming person.

This lovely couple does have one flaw. They are frequently so caught up with what they are doing that they are late for the next activity on the agenda. They were paged at the airport before the plane took off and have been known to follow missed tour busses in an automobile.

The four of us bought tickets for a canal boat tour of Amsterdam. After we bought the tickets we discovered that the boat was full and there would be an hour wait until the next one. We were annoyed. Matt and Happy decided to spend the hour shopping. Verl and I elected to rest our feet and people-watch from a bench by the canal.

In half an hour, the boat arrived and began to fill up. We realized that if we didn't get on, it would be filled and we would have to wait another hour. Matt and Happy were nowhere in sight. I explained the problem of the missing friends to the young woman who was taking the tickets and asked permission to save two places. She assented and Verl and I sat on a bench on one side of a table and threw our jackets on the bench across from us.

The boat was filling. Where in the heck were Matt and Happy? Two attractive women about our age paused by our table. "We want to sit here," one announced in accented English.

I explained that we were saving the seats for our friends and that we had not been able to get on the last boat and had waited an hour.

"But it is not fair that you should keep two good seats when there are no seats for us." There were seats, admittedly not as choice. The woman kept complaining about our unfairness and her voice raised. (Somewhere she had learned that people give in when they are embarrassed.)

Where, oh where were Matt and Happy? "The conductor gave us permission to save these seats. Our friends will be here any minute." Everyone was looking. I could read Ugly American in their eyes.

The woman who took the tickets came back to see what the noise was all about. She said that she had given us permission, but she was soft spoken in the face of the wrath of this assertive woman. The conductor retreated to the front of the boat and left Verl and I to defend the seats. The arguing and insulting went on.

The boat's horn tooted and just before the gangplank was raised, Matt and Happy strolled on, arms laden with packages and faces wreathed in smiles. I doubt if we were smiling when we indicated that the empty seats were theirs.

Matt looked up and down the boat and, seeing only two seats separated by many feet, he smiled down at the irate ladies and said, "It would be a little crowded but would you join us?"

We scrunched together, bracing ourselves against falling off the small benches. Verl and I stared straight ahead.

Matt smiled at the aggressive lady, "My, you speak good English. I don't place your accent. Where are you from.?"

Madam Assertive was from Belgium but she had married a Pole who flew for England during World War II and had lived in England. Her companion was a girlhood friend who was living in Paris.

Interesting woman. I might have liked her if she hadn't been so difficult.

These women were curious about Happy and there were questions about her history. I attempted to join the conversation.

Madam said, "See, I told you there was space for us

here." I gave up.

We saw the world's narrowest house, the bridges and the sights from the canal. Matt and Happy had a fascinating conversation with our new companions.

As the boat docked, I felt Verl's body shaking with suppressed laughter. The humor of this ridiculous situation was stronger than the irritation. My mood lightened, as it always does when I feel Verl's laughter. When we filed out of the boat, we bade our Belgian and French companions a smiling farewell and the four of us hurried down the cobblestone street to buy delft and look at the crazy haircuts the young people were wearing.

If the opportunity to travel with Matt and Happy comes again, we'll take it. There are more important things than being on time.

# 32

## *Cow Plop Bingo*

At times I have wondered if the traditions associated with country life still exist. Are we reaching nostalgically with cute country-kitchen ornaments for a life that is gone? Good roads, fast cars, electricity and communication technology make life in this community much like life in the city or suburbs.

A neighbor's daughter graduated from the Sorbonne. Last week the carpenter who is doing some work for us took the afternoon off to go the the airport to meet his daughter who has just spent a year at the University of Rome. When Verl and I drive the 50 miles to Portland to attend the opera or concert, we meet our neighbors there. Grass farmers keep their records on computers and use modems to check the market. The simple, naive girl, the unschooled cowboy and the country bumpkin exist only in fiction.

At times it seems that, aside from my husband's occupation and the activity at the nursery, I might be living anywhere. Then I read the local weekly paper and decide that yes, country still does exist.

My favorite part of the paper is the Police Report, written in the laconic language of Joe Friday. Here are a few excerpts from *The Silverton Appeal Tribune/Mt. Angel News:*

3:25 AM, Animal complaint, Madison St., Advised that her dog had brought a large opossum into her bedroom. Officer responded.

7:32 PM, Assault, McClaine St., Report of a subject being threatened with a .357 Magnum.

4:16 AM, Assist Public, Norway St. Advised she needed assistance getting her mother back to bed. Officer responded.

The Police Report also includes reports of domestic violence, vandalism, traffic violations and an occasional fight. There is no need to begin classes in community policing here; it has always been practiced.

Unfortunately, the paper frequently contains the obituaries of young people who died in traffic accidents. "Alcohol-related" is the phrase they use to describe the cause.

A recent paper described a remarkable contest that was held in this community, Cow Plop Bingo. In order to raise money for the FFA, Future Farmers of

America, this ingenious gambling game was devised. The local football field was fenced. This is a relatively easy task with electric fencing. One live wire strung between temporary posts will keep any wise animal confined. Then the field was marked off in grids.

The temporary ownership of the grids had been sold to 400 eager gamblers. Next Bossy arrived. Her services had been donated by a local dairy. She tripped daintily down the ramp from the pick-up on hooves that reminded me of the platform soles we wore in the Fifties. Bossy was a young heifer, an adolescent cow. There was no use upsetting a mature milk-producing cow by having her travel to take part in this game of chance. Besides, Bossy was about the same age as the players.

The grass on the playing field was short but succulent. The hills above Silverton contain the best grass seed farms in the world and the community does support high school sports. Bossy looked around a bit. She might have wondered what those crazy people were doing sitting on the bleachers on such a cold, damp day. Then she devoted herself to the work of cows, consuming grass.

On the sidelines, the players watched and waited. They told cow jokes and jostled each other. An hour passed. What was wrong with that darn cow?

Half an hour more. It began to rain. Was she sick?

"Here, Bossy, come over here to my square."

"Scat, Bossy, go back to mine."

"Hey you guys, no fair!"

Finally, an hour and 36 minutes after the game began, it was over. Bossy plopped on Square 146. A cow plop, in case you are from Manhattan and don't know, is an euphemism for the defecate.

The young man who had paid for the square on which Bossy plopped won $350 and the FFA earned $750 for jackets and activities. The readers of the local paper had a good laugh.

And I have proof that "country" does exist.

# 33

## Sunday Inspection

My friends, who visit in the summer, look out across our fields, drink in the stillness and exclaim, "Flossie, it is so beautiful. If I lived here, I'd be outside all the time."

If they were to visit during the week or on most Saturdays, they would have a different view of the nursery. I live in the middle of a factory, a plant factory. Outside my windows, large, orange tractors and small, green ones pass constantly, hauling one, two three wagons loaded with plants. In the summer, as many as three large trucks are waiting to be loaded. In the sheds, where the potting machines stand, ten voices shout rapid Spanish over the sounds of the machine and the portable radio.

If the field that faces the house is rented to the farmer who raises wheat, a huge, green tractor—enclosed cab, air-conditioned, stereo—circles, sending forth clouds of dust. Every other year, when iris are planted there, the field may hold as many as a hundred workers, bending planting and sorting the bulbs.

Now, picture me, or you, sitting out on the patio, reading or contemplating the scene. I'm sure if any of the Protestant Ethnic has permeated your skin, as it has that of most Americans, you would find the display of leisure in the midst of such industry unacceptable. I am just too guilty to enjoy the patio, or take a walk through the back fields when I see so many people working hard.

I spend my days in my study facing the Japanese garden hidden behind a screen of bamboo. The trees planted outside the solarium are tall enough to provide privacy. In the winter, the solarium is a warm space, out of the wind and almost outside. If I sit in the living room behind the glass wall, the workers look in as they go past and wave to me. That is pleasant, but if I receive more than one or two greeting, I begin to feel the creeping pangs of guilt and move my leisure to a less conspicuous site.

On Sundays the nursery is mine. I put on my most comfortable shoes and outer clothing appropriate to the weather and sally forth to reclaim possession of our land. When Verl sees me, he joins me.

"First," he says, "come in the big greenhouses. I

want to show you something."

We tramp to adjoining houses and go inside. Green plants fill the space divided by two aisles stretching 250 feet. Traveling booms spew forth droplets of water as they roll slowly down the walks. Verl runs through the artificial rain to the other end to turn off the irrigation system. Then we stroll down the aisles inspecting.

"Look here, at these roots." He turns up the pot, and with a little shake, dumps the contents into his large hand. The soil keeps the form of the pot. With his little finger, he points out the web of tiny roots that push out from the dirt. "See the micrahizal roots."

A little farther on we admire the callouses that indicate the grafts are becoming part of the plant onto which they have been grafted. Lacy maple leaves are admired. The small bell-like flowers on the kinnikinnick plants are praised. A note of discontent creeps into Verl's voice when he notices the rare graft that is dying or the flat of cuttings that look sick.

We move on to the small glass greenhouse where thousands of cuttings are placed in soil and nurtured in a controlled atmosphere until they push out roots and become plants.

Verl's voice rings with enthusiasm as he shows me his nursery. Because I have a scientific education, he can explain the process of what we are seeing and I understand it. The three English-speaking Mexican workers have an intuitive feel for the plants but no scientific knowledge. Our Caucasian employees are not especially interested in the plants themselves. Verl loves to have an audience and I am happy to be his.

This part of the inspection over we walk down the lane to "the back forty." We pass blocks of beautiful blue spruce trees, some so blue that they reflect the pink of the dawn and the golden sunset. We admire the unusual shapes of the weeping Norway cedar.

On the eastern horizon, the foothills of the Cascade Mountains lie beneath Oregon's changeable sky, and on a clear day, Mt. Hood's snow-covered peak is visible. The foothills are often covered with snow while in the valley snow is rare. In the late summer, the grass seed farms are golden in the distance. The dark-green spikes of Douglas fir mark the boundaries of the fields.

I try to keep up with Verl's pace and am breathless by the time we reach the pond. We stop and admire the water. If we are lucky, we will see wild ducks and geese. Occasionally a nutria will swim past. The land around the pond is too rough to cultivate so it is left to woods. Tall firs and a maze of blackberries hug the banks.

Several years ago, a family of beavers took up residence in our pond. They cut down a maple tree and dammed the water flooding our neighbor's field. Neighboring boys solved the problem by trapping the beaver. Farmers love nature, perhaps more than anyone, but their love is tempered with practicality.

We tramp down a special path to admire the bamboo. Bamboo is Verl's hobby. It isn't a success commercially, but we have more than 40 varieties. This bamboo is Japanese timber bamboo rescued from a restaurant yard one step ahead of the wrecking ball and bulldozer. When they were first dug the 40-foot tall plants were suspended lengthwise in the greenhouse in 100 percent humidity. They were too tall to set upright. When it was apparent that they had survived the shock of being uprooted, they were planted and carefully nurtured. The columns are four inches in diameter and reach up under the fir trees which hold the guy lines that anchor them in the wind. The plants are struggling, but alive in their new habitat. We climb up the bank relieved. If plants are nourished by love, these will surely grow. If this walk takes place in April, we may pick some trilliums near the pond.

We see deer tracks. "What's that smell?" I asked on a recent walk, wrinkling my nose in disgust.

"Oh, it's a little deer. Over in the brush. Someone shot it. Poachers."

"Oh, how could they? A fawn?"

"Yes. They flash the light and when they see the eyes, they shoot. I suppose a baby's eyes shine like an adult's."

No one comes back here on our lane. They must come in through the back across the adjoining farms.

We trudge on, feeling helpless. Even a fence couldn't keep people out of these fields.

When we kept sheep near the pond, a doe grazed with them. I wondered if the dead fawn was her baby, or if she is even still alive.

"Well, at least we have some deer," Verl says. When Shorty lived up in that little house, he poached all the time and we never saw any tracks."

We console ourselves and continue our walk. Verl dashes into the blocks of trees to inspect them closely with the energy and speed of a young man. He delights in telling me how much a certain group of trees is worth. On these walks, I accept the figure and don't deduct the cost of wages, compensation insurance, etc. He reminds me that the veteran's loan agency wouldn't lend him the money to buy this farm because it wasn't large enough to be an economic unit. "Now it supports us and 15 families."

The last part of the walk, back to the house, is up a slight grade and keeping up with Verl makes conversation difficult. I look around at the hills, the straight rows of spruce trees and at my fit and happy husband. And I decide that my friends are right. I do live in a beautiful place.